CANADA
** VS **
UNITED STATES

How Canada is *So* Much Better than America

Jeff Pearce

FOLK
LORE
PUBLISHING

The Publisher: Folklore Publishing
Website: www.folklorepublishing.com

Library and Archives Canada Cataloguing in Publication

Pearce, Jeff, 1963–
    Canada vs. United States : how Canada is so much better than America/ Jeff Pearce.

Includes bibliographical references.
ISBN 978-1-894864-79-4

    1. National characteristics, Canadian. 2. National characteristics, American. 3. Canada—Relations—United States. 4. United States—Relations—Canada. I. Title.

FC249.P43 2010   303.48'271073   C2009-906813-3

Project Director: Faye Boer
Project Editor: Wendy Pirk
Photography credits: Every effort has been made to accurately credit the sources of photographs. Any errors or omissions should be reported directly to the publisher for correction in future editions. Photographs courtesy of Sheng Wang (p.19); Library and Archives Canada, reproduced with the permission of Library and Archives Canada, credit Robert Cooper/Canada, Office of the Prime Minister collection (p. 79, PA-141503); Government of Ontario Art Collection, Archives of Ontario (p. 96); Library and Archives Canada (p. 120, C-009990); National Defence, reproduced with the permission of the Minister of Public Works and Government Services, 2010 (p. 160, KA2004-R101-548.JPG 2004). *Back Cover Illustration:* © JupiterImages | McMillan Digital Art

We acknowledge the support of the Alberta Foundation for the Arts for our publishing program.

We acknowledge the financial support of the Government of Canada through the Book Publishing Industry Development Program (BPIDP) for our publishing activities.

 Canadian Patrimoine
Heritage canadien

PC: 5

Dedication

This book is for Tom Canton and Edgar Fraser,
two of my favourite patriots and creative types,
who I think will most appreciate it.

It's also for my beloved daughter,
Lily, my favourite Canadian.

Contents

Six: History

Seven: Religion

Eight: Sports

Nine: Military

Fifteen: Cool Spy Stuff

Sixteen: Security

Seventeen: Relations

Eighteen: Let's Swap

An Epilogue of Compliments

Selected References

Acknowledgements

I WANT TO THANK ALL THE fictional Canadians who had absolutely nothing to do with this book and who demonstrate that we are nothing like what we think we are: Dudley Do-Right, Bob and Doug McKenzie, Wolverine, Big Bobby Clobber, Don Cherry, Bartholomew "Three Cheers for Me" Bandy, Captain Canuck, Anne of Green Gables, Emily of New Moon, Olivia "Street Legal" Novak, the entire population of Dog River, Saskatchewan, and the horny bear of Marian Engel's extremely annoying, pretentious, subsidized novel.

I also need to thank several real Americans who I wish were made up: Richard M. Nixon, George "Dubya" Bush, Bill O'Reilly, Ann Coulter, Charlton Heston, the membership of the National Rifle Association and a substantial number of the Republican population of Texas—all for their hate and ignorance, which has been unintentionally comical. And sad.

In case anyone is paying attention, I also need to thank Faye Boer at Folklore Publishing for allowing me the unique opportunity to rant, praise, whine and occasionally mimic spontaneous combustion in literary form over how we stack up against the 'Mericans. Many thanks go as well to Wendy Pirk, to J. Michael Cole for taking the time to comment and to Megan MacLean at National Defence for her patience with me.

Any factual errors are unintentional. All insults are deliberate. The reader should understand that my conclusions and any factual mistakes are mine alone, and which I will blame on sleep deprivation, alcohol, Contact C overdoses and, oh yeah, the exchange rate.

Painless Introduction (Honestly): A Canadian and an American walk into a bar...

THIS BOOK DOESN'T HAVE TO BE read from front to back, but as long as you're here...thanks for stepping up to the bar! Pull up a stool and order yourself a beer (a Canadian beer, please—Molson, Keith's, Labatt). It's not that important and you don't really need to know, but this little section tells you why this book exists in the first place and why it is the way it is. You'll soon notice as you go along that the book takes a very deliberate, totally biased point of view in Canada's favour.

Yes, of course, we could try to do a heavily analytical, balanced examination of the issues and elements to determine where Canada is better than the U.S. and where the U.S. outperforms our country. We could grieve over the thought that our culture is perhaps getting eroded by American influence, how our exports need to reach other markets besides the behemoth to the south, blah, blah, blah....But what fun is that?

So as you take a couple of sips and we kick the topics back and forth, don't be surprised if a beaver waddles over and rests his tail on one side of the scale (oops). Not that we won't occasionally take our lumps when we come up short, but this book is a kind of pocket advocate. When Americans bad-mouth us or condescendingly poke fun at us, or even when we occasionally, sadly, bad-mouth ourselves and get neurotic over our drawbacks and failures, this book is here to tell us how the eagle should get stuffed.

And that brings us to the Canadian and the American walking into the bar. It sounds like the start of a joke, and if it is, this book is the punch line. But really, this little volume is ammunition for when you sit over drinks with an American friend (or even a stranger), and shooting the bull turns into a spirited discussion—maybe an outright shouting match at times—of who has it nicer, who has the better country.

It happened to me. In 1992, I was in New York City for a job interview, and I walked into the fabled Whitehorse Tavern. It was a time of heavy election campaigning for the Americans, and a large crowd of patrons gathered to watch the coverage of a debate by Bill Clinton, George Bush Sr. and diminutive Ross Perot (who has now shrunk even smaller as a historical footnote). I struck up a conversation with an American beside me, and before too long, he was adamantly insisting that Canadian health care was no better than that of the now-abandoned Soviet Union, with weary, wretched masses lined up around the block at hospitals, literally dying as they waited. Sound familiar?

"That's ridiculous!" I said. "Look, I'm from there. That doesn't happen." From hoping desperately that I could land the job I'd come to interview for and work and live in the Big Apple (one of my favourite cities in the world, where I always find 99 out of 100 people are nice to me, invite me to pubs and even give me free theatre tickets), I had turned into a patriot on the spot.

The American shook his head like a four-year-old convinced that Santa still exists (and no doubt five years later, he probably denounced Santa as a Commie, since the fat guy wears red). "I'm telling you, my friend came back from there two months ago, and he says it's happening. Folks are dying in lineups!"

"Listen to me carefully," I said, losing my patience but keeping my voice calm and authoritative. "I'm a Canadian citizen. I was born there. I just got off a plane from Toronto. You really think you and your friend know more about a country where I've lived my whole life and where I just arrived from yesterday?"

It was the first time I'd ever seen a human being physically deflate. With an embarrassed look and at a loss for any sensible reply, he literally stopped talking to me and wandered away to watch the television.

Yeah, it was a nice moment. But it would have been better if I'd been armed with some knowledge about how our health care system really works compared to theirs, or if we'd been talking sports, how our athletes are incredible at grand prix racing, baseball, golf, basketball, you name it, not just hockey, or if we'd discussed the environment, how much freshwater we really have and so on. And in fairness to Americans, we don't really know as much about them as we think we do.

A case in point: I had an English geography teacher back in high school who crushed all our Canadian superiority about how "we know more about them than they know about us" by making us fill in a map to identify all the U.S. states. None of us could do it (you try remembering which is Nebraska and which is Kansas when the spaces are blank).

So this is definitely a pro-Canadian book, but it's certainly not meant as an anti-American book (except for one wicked and hopefully delicious part, for which I make absolutely no apology). I happen to like and admire many aspects of American culture, history and business. But I'm also really thankful for what we have here, as we all should be. This volume is meant as a page-turning Pez dispenser of useful information,

11

all in a nice candy-coated, quickly digestible form that lets the educational material go down more smoothly. Unless it's stated otherwise, you can assume all money figures are in Canadian dollars.

I have to give special thanks to editor Wendy Pirk for going the extra mile and compiling data in most of the charts and tables, a Herculean task that was beyond me (it was beyond me because I was fleeing the opposite direction from this homework).

We'll compare. We'll explore. We'll shrug sometimes, but more often than not we'll give three cheers for us.

So next time you're in a bar with an American who is putting down our money, our health care system or our lack of TEC-9 semi-automatics available to 12-year-olds, you can say "Oh, yeah? Did you know that according to the United Nations survey on such-and-such...?"

Because as much as the Americans say theirs is the greatest country in the world (all the time, and Jeez, are they trying to convince themselves of it or what?), up here, we know this is really the best place to be. And we can make solid arguments that it's true.

You're welcome. You owe me a pint.

ONE
Quality of Life

LIVE HERE AND
LIVE LONGER

LET'S START WITH THE REALLY important stuff: living, dying, health and happiness (for happiness, see the bit about sex, page 16). The big news is that just being here is good for you.

What we mean is that being Canadian means having a better chance of growing old—we actually live longer than Americans, and that's according to the CIA's own *World Factbook* for 2009. (Hmmm, at this very moment, perhaps, spies for the Company might be carrying out video surveillance to watch Canadians age in real time!) Americans don't even come close to us as silver foxes—they don't live as long as the French or the British and certainly not as long as those life marathoners, the Japanese. The average American lives only up to 78 compared to our 81 years.

We can also expect more years of good health, free of disability: 73 years compared to 70 for Americans. That might make Americans think twice about condemning Canadian health care (see page 22); countries with the highest life expectancies—surprise, surprise—all have public health care systems.

Our system helps, but it's also how we live. On paper, Americans smoke more than we do—20 percent of their population compared to 17 percent of ours—but we introduced stringent anti-smoking legislation on both federal and provincial levels early on. The Americans don't even have a federal nationwide smoking ban in the workplace yet! And in several states, you can still light up and puff cancer clouds in restaurants, bars and public places.

We Canadians could use a couple more days on the exercise treadmill—in 2007, 15 percent of us admitted to the Organization for Economic Cooperation and Development (OECD) that we were fat. The OECD, being nice, replied that the outfit we were wearing only made us look fat, and that the camera adds 10 pounds (no, not really). But we're still trimmer than Americans—in 2006, 34 percent of our southern neighbours admitted they were obese.

Many experts say who we are as Canadians might also make a difference. We're a nation that's been saying there's room for one more (or a thousand, or a few thousand) for some time now, and naturally, we check how healthy the ones are who plan to stay. When we screen immigration applicants, we also favour those who bring something to the table—and those economically better-off people with good professions generally tend to be healthier.

Add to that what immigrants do bring to the table—as in dinner. Britain demonstrates the point a little more dramatically. Yes, it's still the land of eggs, sausages, boiled tomatoes and baked beans, but these days most Brits will go for tasty and more nutritionally healthy kebabs, Indian curries and other ethnic dishes. In Canada, no doubt, we've also gained by diversifying our diet.

The best news about our improved quality of life is that, hopefully, we no longer get lied to about how out of shape we are, like we were with those ParticipACTION commercials in the 1970s. Remember those? How they claimed a 30-year-old Canadian guy was only as healthy as a 60-year-old Swede?

They made that up.

JE T'AIME IN SNOW
BOOTS WITH MAPLE SYRUP

OH, SURE, YOU MIGHT HAVE left your heart in San Francisco, and it's easy to be romantic when it's autumn in New York. Now sing a sexy tune in Winnipeg when it's −40°C in November! But when it comes to measuring the really important things (ahem), it turns out we're better lovers than the Americans. No, honestly. It's not just us saying that; it's one of the world's leading condom manufacturers, Durex (if you trust them enough to wear their little raincoats, surely you'll listen to what they have to say).

Durex conducted a global survey on sexual habits for 2007–08, and it discovered Canadians are…well, we don't like to brag, but let's say we're more *experienced* lovers. Canadian men average 23 partners over a lifetime, while American males only go to bed with about 13 lovers. And Canadian women are no shrinking violets either—they have at least one more partner during their lives than their American counterparts. Oh, by the way, we don't just beat out the Yanks. We actually do better in Durex's categories than those with Romance languages like the French, the Italians and the Spanish.

Maybe it's because we often start sooner. You can make up your own mind about who has been more backward historically when it comes to sex and the law. Since 1892, believe it or not, the age of consent in Canada was 14 until it was finally bumped up by two years in 2008. But we also have the "close-in-age" exception, which allows 14- and 15-year-olds to have sex with a partner who is less than five years older than him or her.

In the U.S., age of consent depends on where you are. For many states, it's 16, but close-in-age laws can get downright confusing. In California, a difference of less than three years between partners doesn't count as an exception—it simply means you're guilty of a misdemeanour instead of a felony.

We may start at younger ages and have more sexual partners, but we also seem to be more responsible than Americans. We certainly should be applauded for having fewer cases of the clap. For instance, in 2007, fewer Canadians got infected with chlamydia than Americans—for every 100,000 people, 217 Canadians were infected versus 370 south of the border.

We actually lead the world in vasectomies—and it's not just a case of a man deciding to no longer have children. The Population Reference Bureau of Washington found that more Canadian women depend on male sterilization for contraception than in any other country it surveyed. *Maclean's*, wondering why we're such decent guys up north, asked a doctor in Vancouver, Neil Pollock, who told the magazine: "I'm hearing a lot of sensitive comments from patients who empathize with their wives and what they've gone through during childbirth."

But what really makes us the better lovers? Timing. On average, we spend 37 minutes on foreplay— that's more than lovers in any of the other countries surveyed, except for Switzerland. (Yes, yes, I know: Switzerland. They spend 42 minutes, but come on, about two of those must involve yodelling and another five probably have to do with chocolate, which we'll call cheating).

Thirty-seven minutes, Canadians. That's a whole two minutes more than your average American lover. "Two minutes?" says the American with a derisive snort. "That's nothing!"

Oh, yeah? Ask any American woman what two extra minutes can mean in terms of foreplay.

That's right, if she overhears that remark, she's going home with the Canadian.

WE'RE SUUUPERRR!
THANKS FOR ASKING!

OKAY, THAT'S THE CATCHPHRASE of Big Gay Al from America's animated show, *South Park,* but it seems appropriate for what is a Big Gay Country. We wear it, pun fully intended, with Pride. In 2005, Canada became the fourth country in the world and the first in the Americas to allow same-sex marriage.

Queer in Canada means big bucks. Toronto's Pride Week is bigger than even that of fabled gay Mecca San Francisco, bringing in a million visitors each year (Toronto did well even when the city's downtown coped

Pride Toronto, 2006

with a garbage strike in the smelly summer of 2009). Each year, it's pumping more than $100 million into the city's economy. (Honestly, I'm not trying to be suggestive by using the verb "pumping.") And the self-proclaimed Centre of the Universe will host World Pride in 2014, which the executive director of Pride Toronto expects to be "five times bigger" than the annual week-long festival. You better believe that will mean even more cash.

In the U.S, sure, they've had individual states finally get around to legalizing gay marriage—but then a state can rescind this right, as California did with Proposition 8 in 2009, defining marriage as a union between a man and a woman (except for those gay marriages already performed, which are still valid, making for quite a contradiction). This happened in California! The place where everyone assumed anything goes. Nope. And for more than three decades, Florida banned gay men and lesbians from adopting children, until a judge ruled in 2008 that it was unconstitutional—and the state has made an appeal, wanting that ban back in place.

Even President Barack Obama, whom Canadians love for being "sort of like us" when it comes to having a pleasant and polite character and espousing a lot of left of centre views, can't wrap his head around a right that we take for granted for gay and lesbian couples. He'll go for civil unions but still opposes same-sex marriages.

As this book is being drafted, though, Obama *has* promised to get rid of the rather silly and never successful "don't ask, don't tell" policy concerning gay people in the U.S. military (which still resulted in a lot of tell, with well-qualified Arabic translators in Iraq getting kicked out of the services in the middle of a war because of their orientation). In Canada, the sexual orientation of enlisted personnel hasn't been an issue for years. Granted, our armed forces are small, but let's just say our Canadian pragmatism doesn't give much of a damn who you sleep with as long as you're not sleeping when the shooting starts.

In 1992, the Federal Court of Canada ruled that barring gays and lesbians from military service violated the Charter of Rights. Today, many gays and lesbians hold high ranks in the army, air force and navy, and Canadian Forces chaplains regularly bless same-sex weddings on bases. In the last four years, military recruiters have even taken part in gay pride festivals in Toronto, Montréal and Vancouver.

However, Canadian military bases weren't always happy oases of tolerance. Most male soldiers polled prior to 1992 said they'd refuse to shower, undress or sleep in the same room as a gay comrade. An American researcher told the Canadian Press, "The same kinds of rhetoric we heard [in the U.S.] during our debate in the early 1990s and since—that this would never work, that it would undermine morale and cohesion, that the military would suffer and that it's too big a risk—were also heard in Canada."

But a study by the University of California in 2000 (yep, the same California where voters rescinded marriage rights) found no basis for the allegations. Lesbian, gay, bisexual and transgender soldiers reported they had good working relationships with their comrades in arms; episodes of sexual harassment among women declined, and not one assault could be chalked up to gay-bashing. The study concluded that lifting the ban on openly gay members had no bearing on military performance, unit cohesion or discipline.

Too bad that the Obama administration—according to our Department of National Defence—hasn't bothered to phone up Ottawa for any advice on the issue.

DOCTOR, DOCTOR,
IT HURTS WHEN I LIE ABOUT
SOCIALIZED MEDICINE!

ON ANY GIVEN DAY, ACCORDING to certain right-wing proponents in the U.S., Canada is the land of Hitler. Or it's a Communist enclave (it's so hard to keep track). All because we have a universal health care system. Former vice-presidential candidate Sarah Palin, seemingly oblivious to her own hypocrisy in knocking our system, admitted that her family in Alaska had taken advantage of it. "We used to hustle on over the border for health care that we would receive in Whitehorse," Palin told an audience in Calgary in March 2010. "I remember my brother, he burned his ankle in some little kid accident thing, and my parents had to put him on a train and rush him over to Whitehorse, and I think, isn't that kind of ironic now. Zooming over the border, getting health care from Canada."

No, Palin, the word you should be looking for is *hypocritical*. Keep in mind this is a woman who had to get an education in basic history during her election campaign and couldn't even distinguish the surnames of Barack Obama and Joe Biden. Given her chirpy, oblivious gaffes, ignorance really must be bliss.

When America's health care debate intensified, the rhetoric demonizing us reached an almost hysterical pitch. As Uwe Reinhardt, a health care economist at Princeton University puts it, American private insurers and pharmaceutical companies "deployed certain think tanks to find horror stories around the world that can be used to persuade Americans a public health plan in the U.S. would bring rationing."

Unfortunately for these companies, many Americans are sick of their situation and want a change. And

22

many are figuring out that certain lobby groups are speaking in their name but never in their interests. On MSNBC, Rachel Maddow ripped the lid off one group, Americans for Prosperity, which tried to pass itself off as a grassroots organization, one that busses around speakers who have no problem comparing universal health care to the Pol Pot regime and the Holocaust. Maddow told the group's leader, Tim Phillips, "I personally think that you and the folks that do what you do are a parasite who gets fat on Americans' fears."

But the groups will keep on trying. One that's affiliated with Americans for Prosperity shelled out $3.3 million to run a commercial on American television for three weeks that focused on one Canadian horror story, an Ontario woman who blames Health Canada for delays in her treatment.

Too bad that a study by the OECD, plus other independent studies published in the past five years, keep proving the anti-reform zealots wrong about Canada. Yes, we have long waits and our own share of horror stories, but the Canadian mortality rate from asthma, for instance, is one-quarter that of America, and our infant mortality rate is 34 percent lower. Canadians are also 21 percent more likely than Americans to survive at least five years after a liver transplant. A 2008 report for the journal *Health Affairs* says deaths considered preventable with health care are less frequent here than in the U.S. When it comes to low death rates, we placed sixth among 19 countries surveyed, with 77 deaths for every 100,000 people. Guess where the United States ranks in the table?

Dead last. America has 110 deaths for every 100,000 people.

On the heels of the new studies in 2009, Bloomberg went to talk to Donald Berwick, a Harvard University health policy specialist and pediatrician who heads the non-profit

Institute for Healthcare Improvement in Boston. Berwick patiently explained the facts of life. "There is an image of Canadians flooding across the border to get care. That's just not the case. The public in Canada is far more satisfied with the system than they are in the U.S., and health care is at least as good, with much more contained costs."

We do so well that one American has been lecturing us to keep things the way they are. When documentary film-maker Michael Moore flew up to Toronto in November 2009 for a conference, he warned Canadians that we seem to be on a misguided quest to become more like Americans when it comes to health care, and that we should guard against creating two Canadas, one for the rich and one for the poor. Many Canadians, of course, think Moore's film *Sicko* was almost too flattering of our system. But he insisted his fellow Americans are spectacularly uninformed, and that "it's very easy to run an ad on the nightly news about what a Third World country Canada is, and how people are dying on the sidewalk up here because they can't get in to see the doctor."

Let's talk about cost then, since this is supposed to be another reason to avoid imitating our system. The OECD have found that our doctors and nurses provide care at an average cost per person that's *47 percent less* than in American facilities. And we can bring out another study from 2008, this one done by the Commonwealth Fund, a private foundation that studies health care reform, and polling firm Harris Interactive. It learned that 54 percent of chronically ill Americans skipped a test or treatment and didn't bother to go to the doctor when sick because they feared the cost. That percentage was more than twice the one for people in Canada.

It likely doesn't help the stress levels of these Americans to know that if they wanted to change jobs, potential employers could often dig into their past health claims to help decide whether or not to bring them onboard. After all, if a new employee has a serious illness, the cost of treatment could ramp up the rates on the company's privately funded group insurance pool. As a result, many Americans choose to stay in work positions they don't want anymore because of the possible effects to their health insurance and benefits. The whole phenomenon even has a name: "job lock."

Just before Congress achieved the minor miracle of a health care reform bill passing through the House of Representatives in November 2009, 47 million Americans were without health insurance, while 25 million others were under-insured. And a University of Michigan poll found in June that same year that 43 percent of American consumers were already worried about the status quo, that they might not be able to afford care, even with insurance.

They were right to be worried. That same month, the *American Journal of Medicine* did its own study and found the main reason Americans go into bankruptcy is medical debt—it's been a factor in 62 percent of personal bankruptcies. Americans in bankruptcy with medical insurance are most often in debt to the tune of $18,000, while those without insurance are an average of $27,000 in debt.

And yet, the OECD says, on a national level, the U.S. spends far more on health care than Canada does: $7835 in Canadian dollars for each person in 2007. That's 87 percent more than Canada's $4186 per individual. The U.S. also forked over the highest percentage of gross domestic product (GDP) to health care, 16 percent, while we spent only a little more than 10 percent.

That doesn't necessarily mean we've been spending our money the wrong way. It may just mean Americans like more toys. Like the doctors in Monty Python's *The Meaning of Life*, Americans, for better or worse, have always made sure they have a machine that goes "Ping!" The OECD says that, in 2006, America had more than four times the number of MRI (magnetic resonance imaging) machines—26.5 for every million residents compared with 6.2 for every million in Canada (we'll have to ignore the idiocies of statistics that say you can have "0.2" of a piece of medical equipment; get used to it, because such fiddly decimal bits do crop up elsewhere in this work). Okay, so more scanners. It follows then that Americans would be three times more likely than Canadians to get a scan. The U.S. also has 67 percent more coronary-bypass procedures than Canada and performs 18 percent more Caesarean sections.

But that isn't necessarily a good thing. A professor of public health and medicine at Johns Hopkins University in Baltimore, Gerard Anderson argues that technology is "overused" in American hospitals and clinics because doctors have to justify equipment purchases with revenue. He says that back in the 1960s, Canada was about as expensive as the U.S.

"The real difference has been their ability to control technology costs," Anderson says of Canadian health care providers. And he should know—he conducted reviews of health systems for the World Bank, and he developed Medicare payment guidelines for the American Health and Human Services Department. "The only thing the U.S. is consistently number one in when it comes to international comparisons with Canada and other OECD countries is cost."

The World Health Organization declared in 2007 what many of us already knew. We have 20 percent fewer doctors per capita than the U.S. and that problem, combined with our lack of tech resources, has translated into those long lines the lobbyists want to make so much of. And it's true that we do often wait. The Commonwealth Fund discovered in 2008 that 20 percent of chronically ill Canadians waited three months or more to see a specialist.

But we don't wait for everything, as the lobbyists would have the American public believe. The Commonwealth Fund also learned that in both the U.S. and Canada, 26 percent of chronically ill adults got a same-day appointment with a doctor when they were sick. That's the lowest figure for any of the eight countries surveyed.

What may be even more intriguing are the numbers from when the Commonwealth Fund turned its microscope on the American health insurers. It found that private insurance administrative costs are 12.7 cents for every dollar and reach as high as 18 cents for a few companies. In Canada, administration costs are 4.2 cents on the dollar.

And UnitedHealth Group, one of America's biggest private health insurers, posted a net income of $859 million for just its second quarter of 2009, a 155 percent increase over its profit for the same quarter of the previous year. Kind of brings into perspective why private insurers want American patients to dislike Canadian health care, doesn't it?

Which brings us back to that furious debate over reform of the American system, and how some U.S. citizens have been seeing the light, some of them for a while now. Back in 2000, for instance, two staff writers for *The New Yorker* magazine, Malcolm Gladwell and Adam Gopnik, debated the pros and cons of our system in the pages of *Washington Monthly*. But by 2006, Gladwell, the harsh critic of Canadian health care, was quick to point out in his blog that he has since changed his mind. "I now agree with virtually everything Adam said and disagree with virtually everything I said. In fact, I shudder when I read what I said back then."

MEDICINE'S MERRY
PRANKSTER IN AMERICA

IF SOME AMERICANS ARE AFRAID that Canada will infect the way medicine is provided in their country...they're too late. A Canadian physician who grew up in Dundas, Ontario, already got to the Americans first. Indeed, Sir William Osler revolutionized the way medicine is practiced on both sides of the Atlantic, and it's not because he discovered a specific cure for a disease or developed new surgical techniques. Osler is why gawking young interns pepper you with questions about your bowel movements when you're in your silly, backless paper gown simply trying to find HBO on the overhead TV, and he's also the reason why George Clooney looked so haunted with concern in all those close-ups in *ER*.

Osler took medical students out of the classroom and into the hospital wards. Having studied in London and Berlin as well as in Toronto and Montréal, he borrowed the best from the British and the Germans and implemented the internship and residency system of medical training. Lectures had their place, but what really counted were a proper patient history and the physical exam. It was Osler who developed the first course on post-mortems in North America. When medical schools didn't really bother much with autopsies, Osler paid for an autopsy lab at the Medical School of Philadelphia out of his own pocket. As Patrick Watson and Hugh Graham write in the third volume of *The Canadians*, "His classes were so crowded that some students attended by looking through the skylight." Osler was the first physician-in-chief at Johns Hopkins Hospital in Baltimore, and his 1892 book, *The Principles and Practice of Medicine*, became *the* textbook on clinical care for decades.

And yet Osler was no stuffed shirt. A collector of rare books and a prolific writer, he was a practical joker all his life. He had been kicked out of Trinity College, where he was studying to be an Anglican priest, for borrowing a fetus from the medical school and leaving it on the divinity studies side. He wrote a letter under the pseudonym "Dr. Egerton Y. Davis" to the *Philadelphia Medical News*, which took itself far too seriously, convincing its editors that there was a genuine case of vaginismus in which a man had his penis trapped by a constricting vagina (and no, no such thing has happened, in case you weren't sure). In 1905, for his farewell address to Johns Hopkins before he took his position as a professor at Oxford, he suggested that older people ought to be chloroformed as a compassionate form of euthanasia. Some American newspapers didn't have much of a sense of humour and took him at his word.

One of his students would have gotten the joke. He wrote that "among the many virtues of Sir William Osler was his spontaneous, natural and kindly interest in patients and students, and in people in general." The status of Johns Hopkins as a world-renowned medical facility today is largely thanks to the Canadian who insisted for the student of medicine to "take him from the lecture rooms, take him from the amphitheatre—put him in the out-patient department—put him in the wards."

COLOUR OUR
MONEY HAPPY

YOU KNOW HOW AMERICANS LOVE to make fun of the value of our dollar on every U.S. sitcom? And how they love to make fun of the different colours? (Which has always been odd, because for ages, it was easy to mix up a one and a 100 with *their* money.) The next time they try that with you at the bar, you can inform them that we actually have more money in our pockets than they do.

That's right. Do the math with the currency exchange and comparative purchasing power, and the average Canadian household chalks up a net worth of $131,748 against $100,314 for the average American household. Even with the global recession of 2008, our net worth only dropped 17 percent while that of Americans lost almost a quarter at 24 percent.

Perhaps not surprisingly, given the steady sales pitch of the American Dream and the different banking system down there, your average American has a bigger monkey on his back when it comes to personal debt: $43,365. That's almost twice the size of debt a Canadian has to pay off: $25,275.

We spend only 19 percent of our yearly budgets on house and home, while Americans have to sink 34 percent into theirs. We're spending less on our houses and getting more than they do; most of us, 77 percent, have five or more rooms to enjoy. Only 74 percent of Americans can boast that.

Maybe their money's mostly green because of envy.

MONEY PIT,
SWEET MONEY PIT

THIS LITTLE SECTION IS MORE of a time capsule than anything else given that things may be very different by the time this book comes out. But many experts doubt they will be. Consider that RealtyTrac—one of those real estate industry watchers that Bloomberg, CNBC and the rest of the business media depend on to crunch the numbers— expected foreclosures in the U.S. to reach another record for the second year in a row in 2009, with 3.9 million notices sent to homeowners. And it was saying this on December 10, 2009! In 2008, there were 3.2 million homeowner foreclosures. For much of 2009, three loans went bad for every one that was honoured, and fewer than 1.5 million were eligible for President Barack Obama's Home Affordable Modification Program.

One American real estate industry website put the median price for a home in the South at U.S. $151,100 in December 2009, which worked out to more than a 6 percent drop compared to a year earlier. In the Northeast, things weren't much better, with homes going for U.S. $235,400, and remember this is the U.S. eastern seaboard, once the land of stratospheric property prices.

The upshot was that it was supposed to get worse before it gets better.

Only two days before RealtyTrac's gloomy forecast and a few days after those median house prices came out, StatsCan said the average price for a home in *our* major markets was a whopping $368,665 (as of October 2009). The market had an 18 percent jump compared to the year before. We had such a boom in the housing market that

Finance Minister Jim Flaherty threatened to impose measures to make it tougher for Canadians to get a mortgage.

"If we see further evidence that there is excessive demand in the housing market or that there's an indication that people are taking on obligations that they will not be able to handle in the future when interest rates rise, then we will take some action," Flaherty told CTV's *Question Period*. His most likely tactics, he said, would be to "increase the size of the down payment from 5 percent to a higher number, reduce the amortization—bring it down from 35 years to something less." That would get the Bank of Canada off the hook over raising the prime interest rate.

Of course, with our interest rates at record lows, and so many houses in the U.S. now at bargain prices, you couldn't blame Canadians if they considered shopping south of the 49th parallel for a nice investment. But Americans buying a house up in Canada still probably find it far less difficult than Canadians getting their modest little castle down south. Dare we compare? We dare.

AssignmentsCanada.ca tells visitors on its website that "The bottom line is that buying real estate in Canada is very easy." Of course, it would say that, wouldn't it? After all, it's a website promoting Canadian real estate to foreign buyers.

But it's got a point. Most provinces don't have any restrictions on foreign ownership of property, though some do limit the amount of property a foreigner can scoop up. A non-resident naturally pays a higher down payment, and when he or she decides to sell is required to pay an estimate of the tax *before* the sale, an amount equal to 25 percent of the gain. The seller's lawyer holds on to it until the buyer gets the clearance certificate. As AssignmentsCanada.ca points out, "Canada has tax treaties with many countries, including the United States and the UK. A tax treaty is designed to avoid double taxation for people who would otherwise pay tax on the same income in two countries."

As you read through the site's handy little section on "Buying Property in Canada," you discover that not a lot separates the foreigner from the Canadian in buying property here.

Not so when it comes to America. In 2008, the *Vancouver Province* ran a story under the headline "Buying a home in the U.S. could land you in a legal minefield."

The article admitted that most Canadians will be happy once they've done their homework, but it also stated that "People who made a down payment on a house in a planned development have had the developers walk away from the project as local market conditions or credit availability deteriorated. Some U.S. sellers have tried to change the deal at the last minute. And some Canadian owners of U.S. rental property have run afoul of U.S. labour laws."

One of the *Province's* readers warned that under federal law, a U.S. citizen must be hired to do any renovation or chores on the property, even if comes down to something simple like painting your fence or mowing the lawn. Some developers also have a clause in their contracts that give them the first right to buy the house if you decide to sell it within the first couple of years. "And buyers are forewarned that America is the land of class-action lawsuits, where you could fall victim to one or be seduced into joining one. That being said, you will likely make your house purchase using an escrow agent rather than a lawyer."

Good to know. But hey, why would you go live down there when it's so fantastic up here? Haven't you been reading the rest of the book?

POWERBALLS
AND HAPPY DANCES

TO START WITH, THE WAY WE promote our lotteries is so much more appealing than the U.S.'s approach. While commercials in the U.S. have shown jackpot winners rolling in showers of greenbacks, Lotto 649—before it came up with the catchy but goofy "happy dance" campaign—had the best slogan ever for a lottery: "Imagine the freedom." It wasn't an invitation to greed, American style; it was whispering in our ears—think about what you could do with it. (Then inevitably, some shmuck from Winnipeg or Saskatoon wins and tells the camera how he doesn't expect his life to be different—if that's the way you feel, don't play!) The motto for the New York lottery is the less-than-persuasive "Hey, you never know."

You never know? Seriously? That's the best you can do?

We have national and provincial lotteries, and ours run through provincial lottery corporations. In the U.S., there is no national lottery, though Mega Millions and Powerball might as well be national—they're multi-state affairs that fall under both state and federal regulations.

If you go by the jackpot sizes, like so many other things, the U.S. dwarfs Canada. After all, the biggest prize we've seen lately is $50 million for the relatively new Lotto Max. Compare that to the U.S., where it's been possible to win a *huuuumungous* $390 million through Mega Millions or $365 million through Powerball. But if you're greedy, America may not be the place for you. Consider that if you win here, you get that nice over-sized novelty cheque and keep your winnings in a lump sum that can't be taxed (but you do have to pay tax on interest).

In the U.S., the clawback starts the minute you reveal you're a winner, and they give you a choice. You don't get the jackpot after taxes, but before. You can either take a smaller lump sum, which will still be heftily taxed, or you can take an annuity. Powerball, for instance, says on its website that a prize of say, $100 million would be paid over 29 years and 30 payments. "When you see an estimated jackpot annuity prize, we are estimating both sales and what the market's prices on certain securities will be. The annuity jackpot amount and the cash jackpot amount that we announce are always estimates until sales are final and, for the annuity jackpot, until we take bids on the purchase of securities."

Now think about those statements for a moment. First of all, if our math is right, the $100 million spread over 29 years and 30 payments works out to only $3.3 million or so a year. (Only three million a year? I can't live on that, damn it!) Second, we've deliberately discounted the investment interest, because that's a big question. Do you trust Powerball to pick and choose the securities in which to invest your winnings? (You might want to go check the comparison of the banking industry in the U.S. and Canada, page 38).

Whatever you decide to do, Powerball reminds you, "If you take the cash amount (say $50 million), then you pay income tax on $50 million. If you take the annuity (say $100 million), then you pay income tax on the money you actually receive each year. Just like your wages, a withholding amount is required to be taken out immediately."

Ecch, so it turns out they were right in New York. You never know.

Two
Business

ABOUT THAT MELTDOWN—
WHO WANTS TO BE NICE, SAFE AND DULL NOW?

ONCE UPON A TIME, THERE WAS an ant and a grasshopper. The ant was a quiet soul who believed in an organized colony, made sure he had adequate cash reserves and always politely said "thank you," to flies for cleaning up the forest. The grasshopper, meanwhile, didn't feel like storing anything away for winter and was a firm opponent of regulation. In fact, the grasshopper used to float by on the stream in his new Porsche Leaf and make fun of the ant, shouting "Hey! Hey, *loser*! You *do* know those crumbs you're lugging around are only worth 79 percent of mine! Ah-ha-ha-ha-ha!"

The grasshopper got big and fat and put tacky moss paintings on the wall of his tree penthouse as he handed out loans to practically anyone, without collateral. One day, feeling big, he invited the ant over.

"I'm going to do you a favour, my man!" said the grasshopper, swigging nectar and snorting granules of sugar off the belly of a hot-looking cricket. "I'll sell you these collateralised debt obligations—CDOs."

The ant combed through pages of tree bark explaining these supposedly asset-backed securities, but none of it made any sense. In fact, it looked deliberately confusing. "I don't know...looks to me like you got billions of aphids invested in all this, and they're spreading huge risk."

The ant agreed to buy some CDOs, but not too many, and then went away (because curling was on), and the grasshopper picked up a BlackBerry to check his next appointment. But unfortunately, a tree fell in the forest and *did* make a sound. A whole bunch of angry hornets were soon outside—sub-prime mortgages

37

had collapsed, and their hive was being sold. The fat, bloated grasshopper tried to escape his creditors, waddling more than hopping, but was too slow when a large, hungry bird spotted him and gobbled him up.

Uh, let's say the bird was from Europe. Yeah, that works.

Guess who's the ant? The story of how we emerged on top after the economic meltdown of 2008 does, indeed, sound like a fable. Late in that same year, the World Economic Forum rated our banking system as the soundest in the world, followed by Sweden, Luxembourg and Australia, while the poor U.S. ranked in 40th place. The story made headlines around the globe, which sparked all kinds of remarks of glowing admiration and reviews, including from former U.S. Federal Reserve chairman Paul Volcker, who thought his country could learn a thing or two from us in reforming their system. "Canada has done more than survive this financial crisis," *Newsweek's* Fareed Zakaria observed at the time. "The country is positively thriving in it."

It has to be said that the World Economic Forum didn't go over anyone's books very carefully, punching numbers on the calculator. They just called up 75 executives and asked them what they thought of our banks, comparing their comments with those of the suits in corporate boardrooms in other parts of the world. But as any trader on Wall Street or investment banker at King and Bay in Toronto will tell you, market confidence means money. Our business guys have a lot of confidence, which breeds even more faith in us by the international community.

By February 2009, even newly elected U.S. President Barack Obama was blowing kisses our way. "One of the things that I think has been striking about Canada is that in the midst of this enormous economic crisis, I think Canada has shown itself to be a pretty good manager of the financial system in the economy in ways that we haven't always been here in the United States. And I think that's important for us to take note of, that it's possible for us to have a vibrant banking sector, for example, without taking some of the wild risks that have resulted in so much trouble on Wall Street."

So the question might be: Who wants to be nice, safe and dull now?

And our banks certainly do play it safer, more or less, than American banks. Part of their caution isn't necessarily their choice—it comes from our own regulatory system. If you want an international standard for a bank's solvency, you can go by the first Basel Capital Accord of 1988, which required banks to hold no less than $4 in common equity, published reserves and the like for every $100 lent out. American regulators think a bank has good capitalization with a 6 percent ratio. Our regulators insist on 7 percent, but Canadian banks go even further, preferring a higher cushion of cash at 10 percent.

When you have that kind of capital, it impresses the heck out of ratings agencies and international business prospects. When the smoke finally cleared from the stock market tumble and the subprime-mortgage debacle, 4 of the 10 largest banks left in North America—if you go by assets—were Canadian. And with just seven banks in the world hanging on to an AAA rating from the influential Moody's Investors Service, two of them were Canadian: Royal and Toronto Dominion. (Although there have been some grumbles about the way Moody's does its ratings, that's a story for another day.)

We heard a lot about subprime mortgages during the meltdown of 2008, but it wasn't just an American phenomenon, nor should we have felt so superior. Canadian banks weren't barred by regulators from issuing subprime mortgages—they just didn't like them very much. Subprime mortgages make up only 7 percent of the Canadian market, but they are there. And they did hurt us. As the meltdown progressed, Canadian financial institutions took about $20 billion in writedowns because of mortgage-backed securities and the implosion of the dodgier financial derivatives. The Canada Mortgage and Housing Corporation had to buy up $125 billion in failing mortgage assets.

But not one Canadian bank failed. We haven't had a major bank failure in this country since 1923.

Would a Canadian-sized cash pillow have helped break the Americans' fall? Probably not, according to Andrew Coyne, *Maclean's* national editor, who in April 2009 wrote one of the most insightful analyses ever done on our banking system compared with that of our southern neighbour. He argued that U.S. banks still rely heavily on selling mortgages to third parties—securitization in bank-speak—and this has its roots in American banking history. Americans have always chafed at regulation, and they wanted to diversify their assets. "Their traditionally greater reliance on commercial paper markets for funds, as opposed to deposit-taking, owed much to legal restrictions on the interest rates they could pay depositors." When those bad mortgages started to stink up the joint, American banks were eager to sell them so the mortgages wouldn't be a big strike against the banks' capital reserves. A regulator insisting on more hard cash would have prompted even more panic sell-offs.

Canadian banking regulation, argued Coyne, isn't tighter, it's simply different. Canadian banks, for instance, aren't stuck with an albatross like America's Community Reinvestment Act, which forces U.S. banks to offer mortgages to low-income households whether they want to or not. "Where other countries adopt a detailed, 'rules-based' approach to regulation, Canada uses a more discretionary, 'principle-based' approach. The Office of the Superintendent of Financial Institutions doesn't set out a fixed formula for what it considers adequate provision against loan losses, for instance, but it knows it when it sees it—and has the power to step in to compel banks to make the necessary adjustments."

Coyne pointed out that for years, Canadian banks could own other kinds of financial institutions, something American banks had to wait until 1999 to do. As early as 1987, Brian Mulroney's Conservative government opened the door with a deregulation bill that allowed the "Big Five" to go on a shopping trip and collect large investment houses. But whether investment house or bank, our financial institutions all answer to the Office of the Superintendent of Financial Institutions, an independent agency of the Canadian government that reports to the Finance Minister. (If you don't like how your pension plan is regulated, go see them.) Buying up investment houses didn't overextend the banks; it actually stabilized the investment brokers.

The Big Five

CIBC
Royal Bank
Toronto Dominion
Bank of Montreal
Bank of Nova Scotia

Now in the U.S., *what* you are decides *who* looks after you. Depending on whether you're an insurance company, an investment bank or commercial bank, you might have to comply with either federal or state regulators, or both. Keep in mind that there are only 21 domestic banks in Canada, all with a federal charter, all of which have to follow the same rules. There are more than 8000 banks in the United States, answering to different bodies and having different levels of solvency. Twenty-five failed and were taken over by the U.S. Federal Deposit Insurance Corporation in 2008, while close to 100 failed before 2009 ended.

So when it comes to the Canadian and U.S. banking systems, the ant and the grasshopper fable certainly applies. But so does the story of the Three Little Pigs, with Canadian banks—as fee-greedy, ponderous and conservative as they are—being made out of firm brick and stone and not the cheap plywood of questionable securities and straw regulations.

The kicker to our examination of the American system is that even the national regulator of banks in the U.S. isn't quite a government entity—something even Americans forget! They can call it a central bank all they want, but it doesn't look like the ones for any other country.

Up here, we have the Bank of Canada, which is formally a Crown corporation (and by the way, if you're wondering how *Maclean's* Andrew Coyne can know so much about banks, well, sure, he's an award-winning journalist, but his daddy was a former governor of our central bank back in the fifties). In the States, the President appoints the Fed's Board of Governors, but private banks elect members of the board of governors for the 12 privately owned regional Federal Reserve Banks.

"Visit a Federal Reserve Bank, and you'll see that its operations resemble the activities that go on in private business," chirps the *In Plain English* guide to the Fed's operations. We just bet. True, unlike a business, their job is not to make a profit, but even one of the Fed's vice-chairmen has acknowledged that bankers in America never, ever wanted a central bank governed by political appointees, so they came up with a solution that allowed a so-called "independent within government" approach.

Considering how banks in the U.S. have been performing lately, who knows? Maybe American politicians will want to take a look at this aspect, too. But don't hold your breath.

MORE DRAGONS
IN OUR DEN

AMERICA'S 30TH PRESIDENT, CALVIN Coolidge, once said, "The chief business of the American people is business." (Coolidge was typically bland; when he died, Dorothy Parker wisely asked, "How do they know?") America is supposed to be the land of opportunity, where you come to build your personal empire. Canada is supposed to be the land where there's more to Canadian Tire than just tires.

But while we haven't had much of a business reputation beyond the occasional felony-committing newspaper magnate and Nixon biographer (cue sinister music here), Bay Street is slowly snaking its way into the financial epicentres of the world.

It's true we had a slow start. About 25 years ago, the business centres of Canada were as closed as those famous black doors on the cover of Peter C. Newman's seminal *The Canadian Establishment*. You want entrepreneurship? You want innovative thinking? Heck, you want just a decent business loan? You head south for that. Diane Francis, one of the country's top business reporters, chronicled in her groundbreaking book *Controlling Interest: Who Owns Canada?* how five conglomerates and 32 families collectively ran a whopping 40 percent of this nation's 500 largest companies—the families alone owned 31 percent. Our movers and shakers were mostly anglophiles who would be perfectly comfortable and happy in the gentlemen's clubs of London (and some were, since they sought peerages). Not anymore.

In 2008, Francis took a new group portrait of our billionaires and counted them up, declaring in *Who Owns*

Canada Now that our nation is "more of a meritocracy than ever before in its history." She reports we now have an astonishing 75 Canadian billionaires, 56 of whom made their fortunes the not-so old-fashioned way—they earned them. And 28 of those are immigrants.

"Their experiences and backgrounds are as varied as their business models," wrote Francis. "One billionaire lived in a cave in India for months. Another slept on park benches while busking in Europe for a living...."

As Francis reported, our foreign company ownership has gone up from 25 percent to 30 percent, but that statistic looks worse on paper than it actually is. The truth is there's been a drop in government ownership of companies, and other developed nations with open economies have apparently given up similar percentages to foreign ownership.

Are Americans running our boardrooms? More than 20 years ago, our biggest 50 corporations were in the greedy little palms of American, Japanese and European subsidiaries. That's hardly true today. Of the Big 50, 37 are Canadian-owned.

It's not as if the United States didn't have its own foreign ownership worries. Every so often late at night on TV, you can still catch *Rising Sun*, the Wesley Snipes–Sean Connery thriller based on Michael Crichton's paranoid novel about Japanese takeovers. The paranoia about the likes of Sony and Toyota went away, but foreigners still want a piece of America Inc. Between 1994 and 2005, foreign ownership of American stocks and bonds went from 1 percent to 4.5 percent, while ownership of everything from real estate to financial products soared from 3 percent to 13 percent. That's even before Wall Street took a beating in the 2008 recession. Standing next to

Uncle Sam with only a 5 percent increase, we don't look like we've lost our shirt at all, do we?

When rating 183 countries in how they do business, the World Bank puts Canada way at the top, at number eight. Just in terms of starting a business, we're at number two (the U.S., ironically ranking higher overall at four, is at eight when it comes to this).

Maybe another sign—albeit a superficial one—of the growing respect for Canadian business is what's happened with *Dragon's Den*, which looks and walks and quacks like a CBC show but is just the MotherCorp's take on a hugely popular international franchise format that first started in Japan (which had "money tigers"; there's even a loose version of the show in Afghanistan, where you can watch *Fikr wa Talash*, which doesn't translate into anything about dragons, it just means "Dream and Achieve.") When ABC launched their version, calling it *Shark Tank*, they brought in as co-hosts two Canadian dragons: Robert Herjavec, a security software magnate, and Kevin O'Leary, who launched SoftKey Software from his basement and who the CBC described on its promotional website for the show as "opinionated" and "ruthless."

So far, though, *Shark Tank* doesn't have that dragon's bite you get with the Canadian version.

For one thing, as strange as it sounds, the American sharks are too nice.

GOOD FENCES
AND HIGH SNOWBANKS

THERE ARE TWO WAYS TO READ this section: you can either shrug that what follows is awfully familiar (and it is: see page 92), or you can feel a surge of righteous indignation and get your foot stomps out of your system with a loud "How dare they?" Because it really comes back to how you think about Canada and our economy.

During the George Dubya Bush years, Prime Minister Stephen Harper bemoaned, "What has happened is that Canada lost that special relationship with the United States. We increasingly became viewed as just another foreign country, albeit an ally, a good friend, but nevertheless a foreign country. You know, the northern equivalent of Mexico in terms of the border. That isn't just a shift in the view of the administration, that's somewhat a shift in American public opinion as well, which concerns me."

What is amazing is how surprised our prime minister sounds. When all is said and done, we *are* a foreign country, Mr. Harper. And it looks very much like our goods may have a harder time finding their way onto American shelves in the future. In July 2009 alone, the Canada-U.S. trade imbalance was $2.3 billion in our favour, and with America still recovering from the global economic meltdown, politicians in D.C. don't like that. As this book was being drafted, a "Buy American" $787-billion (U.S.) stimulus package bill was working its way through Congress. Under the bill, a construction project such as a new hospital or daycare facility would have to use steel and other materials made in the States.

The bill kept our International Trade Minister, Stockwell Day, busy murmuring soothing words into the ears of the media and the business community. He reported in late October 2009 that the Americans had accepted the "premise" of granting us an exemption in return for Canadian provincial and municipal governments allowing procurement contracts for U.S. companies. Translation: Uhhh, sure, that's a nice idea, we'll look into it, no promises.

Canadian manufacturers were quaking with fear and indignation over the potential impact of the bill. The president of the Canadian Manufacturers and Exporters Association, Jason Myers, argued Canada could still lose if other countries shut out by the legislation decided to retaliate. "We just see a whole lot of areas where the U.S. is becoming more closed, protectionist and isolated in terms of trade. It's not just that it's our biggest market, but we make things together. We are part of an integrated supply chain. It has far-reaching impacts throughout industries."

Although Washington had given out only a modest portion of stimulus money by late 2009, Myers suggested to *Maclean's* that 250 Canadian firms had already lost business. And while Stockwell Day claimed Ottawa and Washington were lobbing proposals and counter-proposals at each other to find a solution to the Buy American legislation, Myers pointed out that the spirit of protectionism ran through several other bills slowly winding their way through the U.S. Congress. One is the Water Quality Investment Act, which he argued could dampen $4 billion worth of Canadian exports. Protectionism has even threatened—shudder—Canada's hockey. Both an American charter airline and a pilots' union went running to the U.S. Department of Transportation, tugging on its pant leg to complain that

Canadian charter flights for NHL teams were cutting into U.S. business. Harper had to appeal to President Obama while on a visit to Washington, and the flap blew over when Air Canada agreed to "an unprecedented level of monitoring and enforcement" of who steps on the flights.

In February 2010, however, Harper's government announced it had managed to get an exemption for Canadian companies under the "Buy American" clause of the U.S. stimulus package. The Opposition Liberals called the deal "pathetic" and "too little, too late," considering that most of the funds made available by the Obama administration had already been spent. The Canadian Centre for Policy Alternatives suggested days after the announced deal that our companies would get only a brief shot at competing for a miniscule four to five billion American dollars in stimulus projects.

But we may be responsible for keeping ourselves in this mess. And when it comes to attitudes about trade, we're not any better than the Americans, privately holding a "Canada first" attitude.

UP WITH FREE TRADE
WHEN WE FEEL LIKE IT!

IN LATE 2008, BEFORE THE BUY American brouhaha, UPS
Business Monitor Canada went talking to small and
medium-sized enterprises in our country. Guess what?
It found that more than half think the trade restrictions
we have on the Americans should be kept—and the
staunchest sentiment came from those enterprises that
conduct international trade and would actually benefit
if the barriers came down!

The attitude was especially high among construction,
retail and, surprise, manufacturing enterprises—that's
right, the sector that's perhaps complaining the loudest
about the tariff barriers the Americans wanted! Now consider that all these small and medium-sized firms make
up 98 percent of Canadian business, and they want to
build nice, high snow banks around our trade while many
Americans want to raise the tariff fences on their side.

Worse, if the numbers are to be believed, Canadian business has been sitting on its hands and not doing very
much about finding other trade partners to compen-
sate for lost Yankee business. Most so-called "advanced"
countries, especially those in Europe, have been bang-
ing on the doors to sell their exports to what are called
the BRIC nations: Brazil, Russia, India and China. BRIC
economic clout is expected to outmuscle that of the G7
before 2030. What have we been doing to get in on that
action? Not much. Only 21 percent of Canadian small
and medium enterprises that export are paying attention
to the Asian market, and only 10 percent are going after
South America.

Now consider that for the second quarter of 2009, for example, Canada's world imports were $89.4 billion, still outpacing our world exports of $87.6 billion. Just so we don't overwhelm you with stats, suffice it to say for the same quarter, American exports increased while their imports went down.

To be fair, the Harper government has shown signs of waking up to life beyond the U.S. economy. Since taking over his portfolio, Stockwell Day has made a couple of trips to Brazil, that powerhouse of the other America. Our exports there added up to $2.6 billion in 2008, which was a whopping 70 percent increase over 2007. Not bad. But our biggest trading partner, according to the Office of the United States Trade Representative, exported $32 billion to Brazil in 2008. We might want to get away from selling our goods to the Americans, but we'll still have to compete against them for those emerging markets.

"This trend of steering clear of the BRIC nations is troubling to us, especially since it appears to be the opposite from what successful entrepreneurs in other nations are doing," complained Ken O'Connell, vice-president of business development for UPS Canada. "Each of the BRIC nations represents opportunity knocking, and it is time for Canadian business to answer."

He told the *National Post* that many of our entrepreneurs shy away from these markets because they feel overwhelmed by the idea of sending big shipments across international borders that have different customs policies. But, says O'Connell, "it doesn't have to be daunting or overwhelming, and there's really no need for significant investment into the establishment of a supply chain."

So we can continue to dance with one partner or learn how to samba with others.

OUR SUDS ARE SUPER,
BUT AMERICANS HAVE MADE HOPS AND BOUNDS

FOR MANY CANADIANS, THERE IS SUPPOSED to be no contest. Our beer tastes better. It's subjective, but this is a no brainer, right? American beer usually tastes weak, and for years, it sometimes even had a metallic taste because it came out of cans and not bottles the way a *true* beer should be stored, right? Right? After all, we've been making it since 1650, when a Montrealer named Louis Prud'homme got a royal decree to go forth and brew. This is the land of Labatt, Molson, Alexander Keith, and you "*am* Canadian," as the commercials keep telling you.

But as it turns out, the secrets of the suds are not so simple. You're still Canadian, but our big breweries are not. In 1995, shareholders were feeling Blue and didn't like the way Labatt was being run, though the company managed to fend off a hostile takeover bid by a Canadian firm, Onyx. But Labatt was eventually guzzled up by a Belgian brewing powerhouse, Interbrew (which has always sounded vaguely sinister, as if it's related to Elsinore beer, the company Bob and Doug McKenzie fought in *Strange Brew*).

Then it was Molson. Yes, today it has those popular patriotic commercials, but back in July 2004, it announced it was merging with America's Coors in an $8 billion deal. When it happened, Karen Molson, a direct descendant of brewery founder John Molson, said, "It saddens me very much to think that the oldest family-owned business in North America is losing its independence."

Only a few years later, however, it was the Americans' turn to cry in their beers...which were going to foreign hands. Belgian company InBev took over Anheuser-Busch in 2008. (The Belgians are invading!) Americans shrugged and went back to sipping Budweiser. So on both sides of the border we have something in common.

Beer

Beer Name	Company	Country
Labatt	Anheuser-Busch InBev	Belgium
Molson	Molson Coors	Canada/U.S.
Sleeman	Sapporo Breweries	Japan
Alexander Keith's	Labatt (Anheuser-Busch InBev)	Belgium
Moosehead	Moosehead Breweries	Canada

But we part company over consumption. If beer was once our favourite beverage, that's changing fast. Canada's beer stores and outlets sold $8.6 billion in suds for the fiscal year of 2007-08, which sounds impressive—until you learn consumption went up only 2.4 percent over the year before. Stephen Beaumont literally wrote the book on our pints, *The Great Canadian Beer Guide*, and he told the CBC in 2009, "Mainstream beer sales have been stagnant or falling for years."

He's right. Beer accounted for 53 percent of the liquor we drank way back in 1993, but by 2008, it was down to only a 46 percent dribble. To get some context with our southern neighbours crushing their Coors cans, we don't even rank in the top 10 of annual per capita beer consumption around the world, and we haven't for years! According to research done by Japanese beer makers Kirin Holdings, in 2004, the real guzzlers of ales, lagers, etcetera were the Czechs, followed closely by the Irish and then the Germans. We're way down the list at number 19, drinking just over 68 litres per year per person. Americans are at number 13, downing six-packs at more than 81 litres per year.

And while yes, we *am* Canadian, we're not always happy to swig a Molson. StatsCan went over the numbers for a study in 2006 and found that imported beers were carving into about 9 percent of the market, more than three times what they accounted for 10 years ago. Today, we can open Kenya's Tusker beer or Ukraine's Slavutych brand. In Toronto, you can walk into a downtown beer garden, and if you're daring, order beer made by Belgian monks that has a ridiculously high alcohol content. Good luck standing afterward.

We can't even turn up our noses anymore at the taste of American beer. "Just as wines from Napa Valley, Sonoma County and Oregon are giving Bordeaux, burgundy and Barolo a run for their money, breweries from California to New York are proving they can make some of the best suds in the world," gushed the *Toronto Star* in 2008. The paper reported there were a paltry 42 breweries across the United States in 1978, while in 2007 that number exploded into 1449. And Toronto restaurants and bars, as well as the Liquor Control Board of Ontario, wanted to stock up on American beers like Southern Tier and the Brooklyn Brewery's Black Chocolate Stout.

"We'd definitely like to have more American beer," the LCBO's category manager for beer, Leanne Rhee, told the *Star*. "Our customers are asking for it."

So it's no longer a competition, really, between Canada and the U.S. when it comes to the suds. We no longer mind who owns our beer or where it comes from, and we make our last call a lot sooner these days. Is that such a bad thing? Not when you consider that with beer...come beer guts.

And we really don't want to win that competition.

THREE

Multiculturalism, Immigration, Passports and Travel

THE RAINBOW
CONFEDERATION

THE *GLOBE AND MAIL* ONCE OPINED in 2005 that "Canada may be the only country in the world where it's seen as good politics before an election to call for a major increase in the number of foreigners who come in." From a political strategy of the Liberals in the 1960s that aimed—rather openly and deliberately—to undermine the Québec separatist movement, multiculturalism has evolved into a Canadian virtue beyond political party lines. We think it's a good thing.

> There are eight immigrants per thousand people in Canada.

So does Mel Hurtig, the bookseller, publisher and encyclopedia creator who has been one our most fervent nationalists and whose books seem to rise in apocalyptic notes of panic with each title (after writing *The Betrayal of Canada*, he tapped out *The Vanishing Country* and then *Rushing to Armageddon*). Although his *The Truth About Canada* in 2008 had the downer subtitle of "Some Important, Some Astonishing and Some Truly Appalling Things All Canadians Should Know About Our Country," Hurtig had a few encouraging things to say about immigration to the Great White North. "As I have pointed out often elsewhere, the brain drain mythology promoted by the likes of Conrad Black and the *National Post* has been grossly overstated. There is abundant evidence that rather than a brain drain, Canada has a huge brain gain, every year, year after year. Between 1986 and 2006, emigration from Canada fell by 24 percent."

Hurtig noted that about 20 percent of Canada's population originally comes from somewhere else, while the average for foreign-born citizens in other countries is 8 percent, with only New Zealand, Switzerland, Australia and Luxembourg having higher rates. StatsCan's 2006 Census found that more than half our immigrants, as we might expect, are coming from Asia and the Middle East. A substantial number still come from Europe, with 10 percent coming from the Caribbean and another 10 percent from Africa.

Percentage of Total Immigration, by Geographical Region (from 2006 Census)

Geographical Region of Birth	Percentage
Asia	60.5
Europe	16.4
Africa	10.5
Other Americas	9.1
United States	2.6
Oceania	0.8

One fascinating statistic from the census was that more people are reporting multiple ethnic ancestries, more than 41 percent. "Increasing intermarriage or unions among various groups has led to an increase in the reporting of multiple ancestries, which has added to the complexity of the ethnic data."

This is StatsCan's excruciatingly dull way of saying something interesting, that Jamaicans are getting with Chinese, while Hungarians might make wedding toasts at a Nicaraguan family home, and wow, what a funky, mocha-golden-creamy-hazelnut frappucino mix our country's becoming! Wow! Hooray for us! As opposed to the poor United States, which still studiously makes sure prime time commercials usually have nice middle class black men paired with nice middle-class black women, because the Heavens might split open if they showed an interracial couple discussing relief for constipation.

Significantly, more people, according to StatsCan, are calling themselves "Canadian" whereas before they might have identified themselves as English, French or Scottish.

This "Canadian example" as StatsCan calls it, along with our "Rainbow Confederation," has probably evolved because these days, once immigrants are here they're ready to join the party. Most of them, 84 percent, go on to become Canadian citizens, and a poll by the Solutions Research Group in 2006 found immigrants consider Canada "the best place in the world" for them to live. They like us—they really like us! And we like them.

Back to Mel Hurtig, who sums up the point nicely: "Almost 80 percent of Canadians believe immigrants have a good influence on our country. In Australia, it's only 52 percent. In the United States and Britain, only 43 percent."

Immigrant Population by Country of Birth (from 2006 Census)

Country of Birth	Number of People
China	155,105
India	129,140
Philippines	77,880
Pakistan	57,630
United States	38,770
South Korea	35,450
Romania	28,080
Iran	27,600
United Kingdom	25,655
Colombia	25,305
Sri Lanka	22,305

That may explain why in annual surveys done by HSBC Bank, measuring how easily foreigners and their families can settle into a new country, Canada ranked as the "friendliest" country on earth in 2008 and the second most friendly in 2009. (We got beat out by Bahrain, which to be fair to everybody, puts a question mark over HSBC's rankings, because they spoke to only 31 expats there!) We rank number two for how easy it is to make local friends and number five for the ability to find somewhere to live. The U.S. is way down in friendliness at number 10, ranking at number seven for making local friends and number 10 for accessibility to housing.

Immigrants, no doubt, have felt that chilly resentment from America, which is why more of them are now staying away from the Land of Opportunity and coming to us. In 2000, there were 647,000 legal permanent residents putting down roots in the U.S., but four years later, that was down to 455,000. Canadians have also been staying home or emigrating to spots other than the U.S.; or perhaps they simply couldn't get in. Our dwindling presence south of the border is a trend that's almost a century old. In 1930, more than 1.3 million Canadians lived in America, but by 1960, that was down to 953,000. By 2000, there were even fewer Canadians, only 678,000.

Do the math, and it looks like that figure is still in sharp decline. StatsCan reported in March 2008 that between 2000 and 2004, an average of about 68,900 Canadians left for the U.S. every year. If we're not experiencing a brain drain as Hurtig argues, we can at least say the Americans get a brain trickle—we certainly look smarter when we show up next to our American cousins. Over half of Canadian-born residents in the United States aged 25 or older had a university education at the bachelor level or higher. That compares to just over a quarter of Americans.

But we still like going down there permanently more than they like coming up here—only 6100 Americans obtained permanent resident status in Canada during the same period. In 2006, we got a few more—11,000, their highest rate for emigration here in 30 years.

Unlike our new arrivals from Africa, Asia and the Middle East, however, most of these Americans make lousy converts to the Canadian way. Only 32 percent of those born in the States who have lived in Canada for more than 30 years chose to become Canadian citizens. Perhaps a column in *The Atlantic Monthly* in October 2009 by Wil Wilkinson provides a clue to this attitude. Wilkinson wrote a chirpy little piece on how he inherited our rights and privileges thanks to Bill C-37, an amendment to the Canadian Citizenship Act, which returned citizenship to those who lost it by taking on a new nationality.

"I work for a libertarian think tank, and libertarians are supposed to disdain the land of poutine and Dan Aykroyd for its socialist health care system and general failure to really love liberty," explained Wilkinson, before gushing, "Yet not only can you get gay-married in any of the provinces, or almost-legally toke up in your toque up there, but Canada's economy is also slightly freer than that of the global hegemon to its south."

Then Wilkinson pees in our snow bank by adding, "But even more important to me is the conviction—a libertarian conviction, I believe—that crossing national borders ought to differ little from crossing the imagined line between Iowa and Minnesota. That's really why I'm so keen about being Canadian. I want my own boundaries to widen, as I'd like everyone's boundaries to widen. Also, I can now put the Canadian flag on my backpack."

You ever get the feeling sometimes *they just don't get it*?

EVERY PICTURE
(AND STAMP) TELLS A STORY

ACCORDING TO THE U.S. STATE DEPARTMENT, only about 30 percent of Americans have passports, while in Canada the
average is closer to 54 percent.

You'd think our estimate would be a little higher, given
that more Canadians travel to the United States than
Americans come up here, and while most of us drive
down, we take our passports to airports. We always had
to, given the sour suspicion of border guards and the grim
possibility we could be turned away. Passport Canada
says it now gets 4.8 million applications a year, which is
a substantial chunk of our population. That compares to
13.4 million Americans needing a passport or passport
card out of a population of a whopping 300 million.

Ironically, once upon a time, Americans probably had
more passports than Europeans. More than 1,184,000
passports were issued to U.S. citizens between 1912 and
1925. But Europeans could and often did travel freely
without documents into the early 20th century. What
changed things? World War One—and the victorious
Great Powers redrawing the maps of Europe, Africa and
the Middle East.

Of course, with the Western Hemisphere Travel
Initiative that came into effect in 2009, both Americans
and Canadians now have to have passports or photo ID
documents to cross into each other's country.

Yes, much of the effort grew out of paranoia in the
wake of 9/11, and yes, we had it really good for a long
time being able to traipse across the U.S. border with
a wave and a smile and no documents after we leave,

61

say, Fort Frances, Ontario (because it's a hell of a lot easier to detour into the States if you're driving to Winnipeg than taking the scenic Ontario route).

No more. And you know what? All of this is a good thing. Why?

Because it doesn't matter how much we have in common, we're still a separate country.

If you fly over to Europe, they use the common currency of the euro. There are more than two dozen countries that belong to the same trading block. Most folks speak at least two languages and sometimes three or more, and you can go from Paris to London in three hours through a tunnel running under a narrow channel of water—but you *still* better bring your passport. They don't care if you came from next door; cough up the papers, mate.

In France, a shopkeeper does not take American dollars, and he would be insulted if you tried to thrust some into his hand instead of euros. It begs the question why our own retailers are so spineless in accepting green-backs from tourists when the exchange rate is mildly in their favour, which only further devalues our currency. (If you think this isn't a serious issue, go to Third World countries where the U.S. dollar is the black market coin of the realm, and where it will be a loooooong time before their own paper can compete; if you don't want us to be thought of as a "Northern Mexico" as Stephen Harper complained, make Americans use our money when they're here!)

The case can be made for a North American version of the euro. The original hasn't made Belgium any less Belgian or Italy any less Italian. But as in Europe, yes, please, let's keep passports for both sides of the traffic.

BEHIND THE MYTH...
IS THE MYTH

KATY STEINMETZ, A REPORTER FOR *The Columbia Missourian*, wrote a column for its website in late 2008 on the supposed myth of the low number of Americans with passports, saying she wanted to "take the opportunity to discredit it, once and for jolly all." Steinmetz had come back from three years in the UK—or maybe from the UK of the 1940s, because no one there uses the word "jolly" anymore, unless they're on the *Balamory* kids show.

We're picking on this one American's recent column because it showcases the whole debate over American insularity so well. She writes: "The loaded assertion behind the myth is this: Americans, the perpetuator suggests, are happily isolating themselves from the rest of the world in the laziest of ways, revelling in cultural ignorance and scoffing at the very idea of going abroad. They could travel if they wanted to, the assumption goes, but they simply don't."

Steinmetz goes on to complain about an article that same year in *The Guardian* newspaper by John Patterson. Patterson, she claims, had called Americans "ridiculous, paranoid, pathetically insular and grotesquely self-pitying." Only he didn't—more about that in a second. Steinmetz complains: "And just so we didn't worry that any of this was hyperbolic, he explained that Americans 'have no reason to hate or fear (foreigners), but they have given the rest of us a million reasons to hate and fear them.'"

The problem is she has taken his words completely out of context. As nasty as Patterson got in his piece, he was actually writing about the latest villain *du jour* trend in

American movies: the foreigner, who is the bogeyman for films such as *The Ruins* and *Turistas*. He was referring to the trend, and this is what he actually wrote: "This is hysterical, of course: ridiculous, paranoid, pathetically insular and grotesquely self-pitying. Americans are right to shudder when they see contractors strung up in Fallujah, but since when have their fellow citizens been tortured or murdered in, say, Dijon or Dusseldorf?"

Ms. Steinmetz spent three years in the motherland of English, which is her native language, I presume, and still can't read.

Her case for so few Americans not going abroad comes down to the family chequebook. Let's give her the benefit of the doubt about the numbers, because she pegs housing at costing Americans in the 30 percent range, based on Consumer Price Index figures. Then you've got kids, car insurance, health care costs in the thousands, blah, blah, blah. Now if you go back and check our section on personal wealth (page 30), you'll see Canadians have $30,000 more on average in net worth, and we pay only 19 percent of our budgets on our homes. Most of us also don't have the anvil of health care costs to weigh us down that Americans do.

But Steinmetz's logic is specious. The fuzzy notion that Americans don't have enough money to travel abroad has become so accepted without challenge that you see it on the WikiAnswers website. Boil it down, and in her article, Steinmetz is basically saying Americans don't travel because they don't manage their money properly and haven't been smart enough (until recently) to get a better health care system. Whose fault is that?

She points out correctly that a flight across the Atlantic can run a family into the thousands. Then she takes the point too far into fantasyland. "Meanwhile, Europeans can fly to Barcelona, Belfast or Berlin for less than a swanky dinner in London town would cost them."

Umm, except they can't ("London town?" Cor! Blimey! And other archaic, unused expressions). This sentence above is just too cute—Steinmetz has made it a link to the site for Ryanair, which yes, offers flights for £5 to the cities she lists. And she still can't read, because as any seasoned traveller over the age of 16 knows, you better click on the airline's link for "Terms and Conditions" and read the one that reminds you "Fares don't include optional fees/charges."

Oh, and by the way, the cost of a "swanky dinner" in London will vary for Europeans just as it will for a couple or a family in New York and Chicago. She neglects to factor in that Europeans also need to pay for gas, parking fees and babysitters, and they must also pay for passport applications before they go on trips, even within the EU.

Canadians have the same oceans separating them from sunny beaches in Thailand and cafés in Barcelona. We still travel. While nearby Mexico was our first locale of choice in 2008, with Cuba third and the Dominican Republic fifth, our second place to fly off to was the UK, and fourth was France. We also went off to visit—in order of popularity—Germany, Italy, the Netherlands, China and Spain. According to StatsCan, we spent $3.1 billion in overseas countries in 2009. Yes, we have more money in our pockets than Americans, but one could argue that given the state of our airline industry, our debatable competitive choices and our purchasing power against international exchange rates, the Americans have far less excuse not to see the world.

Many of our southern neighbours do travel, though. In 2006, for example, two years before Steinmetz's article, more than 63 million Americans went on international

65

trips. Mexico was their first destination of choice, followed by Canada. After that, the order of popularity goes the UK (which the travel industry attributes to it being "familiar" for Americans), France, Italy, Germany, Jamaica, the Bahamas (the Caribbean offering more of the "familiar" say the experts), Japan, China, Spain and the Netherlands.

"The 50 states may share a federal government, but that doesn't mean they're not as culturally and geographically disparate as many European countries," writes Steinmetz. She rattles off "Innuits" (sic) in Alaska, "those who only speak Spanish" in California and people cooking Creole dishes in Louisiana among others as examples of that cultural and geographic disparity. It's a peculiar and uniquely American reasoning, as if the novelty of language or cuisine equates with the educational experience of going to a land that had nothing to do with yours from the start, with people who probably don't think like you.

You can visit Québec, and you will be very sure you're in a unique, distinct culture, but as much as there are still some who would like Québec to be its own country foreign to Canada, it's not. Its whole history is affected by Canada, and there are countless Anglos who have never bothered to learn French in Montréal—all there to remind you that you're *not* in such a disparate land. It's not and never will be the same as going to France, just as if you visit Hispanic sections of California, you can't fool yourself that it's the same kind of experience as flying over to Catalonia.

Steinmetz wrote she didn't expect foreigners to abandon a "Yank-bashing fad." But then if she thinks visiting a corner of her own country is like flying across an ocean to a foreign land, we probably can't expect her to wrap her head around the idea of examining her assumptions more closely.

FOUR

Environment and Natural Resources

MMMMM...
FRESH PINE SCENT!

OUR ECO-FRIENDLY IMAGE TOOK quite a beating at the United Nations climate talks in Copenhagen in December 2009. Critics did everything from threatening to kick us out of the Commonwealth to one environmental group calling us the world's biggest environmental offender at the talks and giving us a "Colossal Fossil" award. Their slings and arrows weren't without cause. Long before the Copenhagen talks, Ottawa missed deadlines on progress reports and updates required for the international community under the Kyoto Accord. Plus environmentalists knocked the Harper government for cancelling programs they say helped reduce greenhouse gases.

It didn't help our international prestige either that Prime Minister Stephen Harper was left off the invitation list when President Barack Obama had an emergency meeting with other world leaders in the Danish capital over climate change. Harper had to settle for a private lunch with Obama the next day. And, while at Copenhagen, the U.S. offered to help raise $100 billion a year for the next decade so more vulnerable nations could cope with our gradually roasting planet; Canada's Environment Minister, Jim Prentice, said Ottawa would contribute to a climate-aid fund, but he didn't give out any hard numbers. In the end, as everyone remembers, the accord in Copenhagen—one that only *some* of the leaders agreed to—wasn't even legally binding after 13 days of debate.

So how do we stack up in terms of natural resources and our environment when compared to the U.S.? America has been a favourite target for environmentalists in the past; in Denmark, Harper's government was the green lobby's whipping boy. To be fair, however, it was Harper's government that in 2009 expanded the Nahanni National Park Reserve in the Northwest Territories.

Protecting more than 30,000 square kilometres, the Nahanni is now almost seven times the size of the original park established in 1972, and it's more than three times bigger than America's Yellowstone National Park. The expansion gave it the highest mountains and biggest ice fields in the Northwest Territories. The park is already a UNESCO World Heritage site and is home to 500 grizzly bears, two herds of woodland caribou and various other species that need protecting. Definitely, a good thing.

THE FOREST
THROUGH THE TREES

OF COURSE, THIS IS CANADA, where the forestry industry learned long ago it couldn't just cut down everything in sight and leave us a barren wasteland. Consider that Avrim Lazar, CEO of the Forest Products Association of Canada, told an industry conference in Buenos Aires in 2009 that he backs the World Wildlife Fund's campaign against global deforestation and says it could go further in calling for a ban to illegal logging.

"Communities that earn a living from the forests are compelled to manage them sustainably," said Lazar. "Canada understood this many years ago, and that is why today we have no net deforestation and no illegal logging in our country. As the world's largest forest products exporting nation, we depend too heavily upon the health of our forests to put them at risk."

Canada's forests are good for a $65-billion per year industry that's responsible for 11 percent of our country's gross domestic product in manufacturing. It also provides almost 250,000 direct jobs across Canada. It hasn't been doing so well lately, with 200 Canadian mills having closed in 2008 and 2009, costing 50,000 jobs, but more about its economy in a moment. Back on the plus side, we've apparently kept 90 percent of our original forest area.

According to Lazar's association, our forestry industry has reduced greenhouse gas emissions by 60 percent (10 times Kyoto requirements), while boosting production 8 percent. Lazar also claims ours is the first forestry industry in the world to commit to becoming carbon neutral through the supply chain—without the purchase of carbon off-set credits—by 2015.

That all sounds well and good. Issue resolved? Mmm, no.

One environmental group in New York, the Natural Resources Defense Council, doesn't make much of a political distinction in criticizing how the industry is "laying waste to North American forests," though it mainly blames top American manufacturers. While the group concedes that "Cascades, Canada's second largest tissue product manufacturer...meets 97 percent of its pulp requirements with recycled fibre," it argues, "Many large tissue producers use trees from Canada's boreal forests and buy pulp from companies that harvest trees from the boreal. The majority of the at-home products these companies produce—brands consumers find in grocery stores and other retail outlets—contain little or no recycled content at all." Not so good.

The Council claims that clear-cut logging for these firms is eating its way through half-a-million acres of Ontario and Alberta boreal terrain that's home to lynx, bear, wolves and songbirds and is "one of the world's largest terrestrial storehouses of carbon dioxide [which plays] a critical role in preventing global warming." It also says the forests of the southeastern U.S. are vanishing at an alarming rate.

Interestingly—though perhaps not surprisingly—green in conscience and green for the so-called "bottom line" have now more than ever grown to be interconnected. Funny how that happened. And how convenient it's been for some.

This is how the log rolls lately. American paper and forest firms have been doing a lot better financially than their Canadian counterparts. In the third quarter of 2009, our largest companies lost $632 million. But in America—which likes to routinely bash our industries, including forestry for "subsidies"—firms were carried along by what's been a $7 billion wave in tax credits, and they posted earnings of $1.2 billion for that same quarter.

71

The tax credits were for burning what's called "black liquor," a by-product of pulping that generates heat and energy. American mills get a grant of 16 cents per litre on the black liquor that powers their boilers, with the size of the rebate dependent on the volume of black liquor a mill produces during the year. As Gordon Hamilton reported in the *Vancouver Sun* in 2009, black liquor "has reduced [American] costs by $200 a tonne, turning unprofitable mills into the world's lowest-cost producers overnight. It has resulted in extreme distortions in pulp and paper markets."

Craig Campbell, of PriceWaterhouseCoopers' global forest and paper industry practice, told the *Victoria Times Colonist*, "If you peeled that tax credit back, U.S. companies would be in the same ball park as Canadian companies." Ottawa countered the huge U.S. tax credit with its own billion-dollar aid package for our pulp and paper companies in the summer of 2009, one designed for green energy and environmental improvement projects. Some in our industry were encouraged by the move, which they understood relies on a "safe harbour" clause in the latest (2006) of the interminable softwood lumber agreements we have with the U.S. The clause allows government funding for managing, protecting and conserving the environment—as long as it doesn't affect timber prices.

Even before Natural Resources Minister Lisa Raitt opened her mouth in Parliament to formally announce the aid (reporters learned about it ahead of time in a media advisory), the American lobby group Coalition for Fair Lumber Imports accused our side of violating the agreement. It complained that this kind of investment is only supposed to go to the forestry industry.

Never mind that their pulp and paper industries get billions in subsidies. They did a great job of raking the leaves over that embarrassing fact.

WATER, WATER
EVERYWHERE, AND OIL...FOR NOW

CANADA HAS A STAGGERING 20 PERCENT of the world's fresh-water reserves—yep, that's right, the entire world. Ummmm, just one catch—most of it is up north, and you might have noticed, uh, well, we're all down here, closer to the 49th Parallel. When we finally get around to the actual Great White North, we won't want just the minerals or oil as goodies, we may want to make sure we can flush our toilets one day with what's up there. It would be nice if we can figure out how to do it soon, since scientists say yes, we have water, but lakes have been retreating and river flows are down. If things keep up the way they've been going, we may have to call Manitoba the land of 100 lakes.

You better believe Americans will want to visit our taps as well. In the summer of 2009, America's largest reservoir, Lake Mead on the Colorado River—which by the way, supplies all the water for Las Vegas 50 km away—dropped to 43 percent capacity. Most of its water comes from snowfall in the Colorado Rockies, which has been down, and researchers say if both climate change and water use habits continue in their current trends, there won't be much of a lake left by 2020.

Then there's California, which relies on the snowpack of the Sierra Nevada Mountains for its water. But climatologists expect the snowpack to drop by possibly as much as 70 percent by mid-century. It's already been down to about two thirds of its normal size, and the state's population of 36 million keeps growing.

If most of our freshwater is locked in ice and snowpacks in our north, and the Americans are getting less water

73

from the snowfall on select mountain ranges, it kind of puts a whole new perspective on that Arctic sovereignty thing, doesn't it?

It's not just water. You name it, we got it: minerals, uranium.... In 2006 alone, Canadian mining was responsible for $70 billion in export income. Then there's oil. The U.S. imports more oil from Canada than from any other country: 19 percent of its total from foreign suppliers.

IT'S THE PITS

IF YOU THINK OUR REPUTATION as an environmental paradise is unblemished despite the Copenhagen talks, we have three words for you: Alberta oil sands.

The Alberta oil sands export about half their production of 1.2 million barrels a day south of the border. The Canadian Energy Research Institute in Calgary expects that over the next quarter century, production will reach four million barrels per day, still with most of it headed south. That could bubble into 380,000 new jobs and another $1.4 *trillion* in gross domestic product for Canada. The Institute has also calculated that it'll mean $252 billion in tax revenues, of which Ottawa will scoop up more than half.

It also means scores of trees being cut down and tonnes of peat and dirt being stripped away in open pit mines in the Athabasca Valley so that valuable deposits of bitumen, heavy crude oil, can be reached—leaving us with a black, gloppy, disgusting and very toxic mess. Even *National Geographic*—a magazine that's offered virtual love letters to our Canadian wilderness in the past with lush photo spreads—put out a fairly critical article on the sands in its March 2009 issue. "Clawing and cooking a barrel of crude from the oil sands emits as much as three times more carbon dioxide than letting one gush from the ground in Saudi Arabia," scolded the magazine. It had to concede, however, that the oil sands make up only one-tenth of one percent of global carbon dioxide emissions.

Sounds like no big deal, but it's going to be. The oil sands are our fastest growing source of greenhouse gases, and they're expected to account for 12 percent of our national output by 2020. In case you're wondering

75

what that output is, it was in the neighbourhood of 747 megatonnes in 2007 alone. Yeah, sure, everyone knows the U.S. was for years the major producer of CO_2 until China got the dubious honour of producing even more than America. But 747 megatonnes in one year? Remember how small our population is at the moment, yet we're churning out all of that. Yep. We better look embarrassed.

But for some, the real threat to the environment both up here and in the United States is an old enemy: coal. Alberta is the only province still building coal-fired plants, and a new one near Edmonton will start operating in 2011. Scientists fear it'll pump out way more carbon dioxide than any oil sands project.

There are those, of course, who want to clean up coal's dirty face. In late 2009, Ottawa and the Alberta government announced they'd pony up $779 million for a carbon capture and storage facility west of Edmonton. The big bucks will help TransAlta retrofit one of its coal-fired generation plants with the new carbon capture technology (it works with a chilled ammonia process, in case you're wondering, and that's as technical as we want to get about it). The gas will then be used for enhanced oil recovery in nearby conventional fields or be buried about three kilometres underground. And almost a million tonnes of it may be buried each year.

It'll be a while before the plant gets retrofitted, and critics have been scratching their heads, asking publicly why a big multinational company needs our money to clean up its act (plus it gets to use the plant improvement for getting more oil out of its fields). That's assuming this technology works the way it's supposed to.

But coal is really king in the United States, which can boast the largest reserves in the world and has more than 600 coal-fired power plants, spewing almost two billion tonnes of carbon dioxide a year, about 27 percent of America's total production of greenhouse gases. Those emissions are likely to rise by a third over the next 15 years.

The *Washington Post* pointed out America also has many "clunkers of the power-plant world"—old generating plants, some located in urban areas of cities like Detroit, Cleveland and Chicago—that were exempted from requirements to use pollution control technology under the Clean Air Act of 1977. And as they've been patched over and rebuilt again and again, critics charged in 2009 they could still squeak through requirements of new legislation over carbon reduction, though some energy experts suggest companies would probably prefer to retire such aging plants.

Environmentalists in the U.S. had a chance to cheer in 2008, however, when the state of Montana pulled the air quality permit for a proposed coal-fired plant, and one utility chose to shut down two of its own plants in Colorado, with the encouragement of regulators in the state. So as much as Americans love their coal (and their electricity even more), there are still some individuals with a tree-hugging, almost downright Canadian streak of conscience who are demanding alternative power sources to plug in.

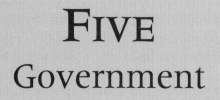

FIVE
Government

CHECKS, BALANCES
AND SOBER SECOND THOUGHTS

OUR GREAT SCOTTISH DRUNK Sir John A. Macdonald once said, "The great evil in the United States is that the President is a despot for four years. Under the British constitution, with the people having always in their hands the power and with the responsibility of a Ministry to Parliament, we are free from such despotism."

Time has proved him right. Yes, Americans can rightly point out that while they've had a Constitution all written down for more than 200 years, we didn't get a formal one, let alone one kept in our own country, until 1982 when Pierre Trudeau asked the Queen in so many words, "Umm, mind if we get this dusty thing out of your desk drawer? We think we can take the training wheels off now." Meaning the British North America

Prime Minister Pierre Trudeau getting the Queen's sign-off on our Constitution

Act, plus all the other papers forming an untidy package that has meant rule of law in this country. Of course, Americans, while considering their Constitution a "living document" that evolves, either don't know or conveniently forget their Founding Fathers hastily scribbled in some revisions so their kind could hold onto power (see page 113).

Our system works better. Honest. No, really, quit laughing.

If I have to stop this book....

Keep in mind, when it came to legislative efficiency and avoiding stalemates that could erode the confidence of citizens, John A. Macdonald had vision. (It might have been blurry sometimes from all his imbibing, but it was there.) Our first prime minister, after all, had a background in constitutional law and understood how states' rights had ripped America in two for a bloody civil war. He believed in federalism and knew the power of parliamentary governance.

Let's walk through their system and our system.

HIS MAJESTY
GEORGE WASHINGTON

NEITHER OF US VOTES DIRECTLY FOR our leaders. Since our system is pretty straightforward to understand, let's start there. You know the drill. You vote for an MP and if he or she gets in, congratulations! You've just given someone a job in Ottawa for more than $150,000 annually, plus a yearly allowance of $22,000, plus 64 free return airline tickets. Oh, and this person is also supposed to represent you in a federal legislature. If enough members of his party get elected, they form a majority, and their top dog—presuming this person also won a seat—gets to be prime minister and be blamed for everything from job losses to lack of swine flu vaccine to however the Americans are treating us that week.

The prime minister can stick around as long as the party's willing to have him, and for as long as his local constituency voters will have him (but since he is bound to run in a nice, safe riding, which always likes the idea of having the PM as their MP, he is usually okay on that score). If he hangs around too long and gets bored and sick of the job, he might take a walk in the snow late at night (Trudeau) or may quit but drag out the farewell by flying around on our dime, visiting old friends and oh, say, shooting boar with Boris Yeltsin (Mulroney), and not be willing to move out of 24 Sussex Drive until his own new private house is ready, forcing the replacement (Kim Campbell) to look like a schmuck and go live in the PM's summer residence.

But like Macdonald said, if we as a people get fed up with him and his party, we can always vote for new individual MPs. The prime minister isn't our head of

81

state. Our head of state is an 84-year-old Corgi-loving grandmother of mostly German descent who lives across the Atlantic Ocean in London. It sounds silly, but there's a huge advantage to this state of affairs. As popular as a prime minister may get, Canadians have never built a lasting "cult of personality" around our leaders, always keeping a critical, questioning eye on them—which is one check on any abuse of power launched behind a flag waved in our faces and the prestige of office. "Minister" originally meant "servant," and a prime minister can never really forget he works for us because he's accountable during Question Period in the House of Commons on a regular basis.

There is no regular Question Period for an American president. But he does get a seal. He even gets his own anthem, *Hail to the Chief*. The job comes with a huge security detail, a private jet with its own name, and when he's done, what's turning into a rather obligatory library named after him (though it's questionable whether a couple of these presidents bothered to read much). An aura of grandeur has been built around the president because he has to be both head of state as well as the head of the government.

This aura is ironic because of the schizophrenic attitudes of the American Founding Fathers. Some were intent on making George Washington a king, which he ultimately refused (but word is he actually considered it), though John Adams still fretted over referring to Washington as "His Excellency" in the Senate and Adams' wife, Abigail, called him "Your Majesty" at a formal dinner. Others came up with the checks and balances system that meant the president couldn't introduce bills in Congress, even though he can sign off on them or veto them. And even though he's responsible for foreign affairs, he can't formally declare war.

But the argument can be made there's a heck of a lot more transparency in our system than theirs. Yes, we don't really vote for the PM (unless you live in his riding), but you might as well be if you choose your local candidate that belongs to his party. So your choice at election can be based on liking your MP, liking the party or liking the top candidate. You still know what you're getting.

If you're an American, you really don't get to vote for the president at all! You go through the wonky Electoral College system.

That means you vote for a slate of electors chosen by the state political parties, which are usually positions handed out to the party faithful. Each state can select a number of electors that equals its total of senators and representatives in Congress (the District of Columbia gets three thanks to a unique amendment back in 1961). The members of the Electoral College are elected every four years under rules established by the legislatures in each state. Forty-eight states require what's called the "winner-take-all" system for presidential elections, so that the largest number of popular votes ensures that candidate gets *all* the state's electoral vote.

This is why, in every election, you always hear about candidates focusing their attention on the states with larger populations.

Still with us? Amazing if you are. Because now we come to the big problem, and it's worth quoting an actual, highly popular textbook, *American Government*, to demonstrate it's not just our prejudice: "The Electoral College has the potential to produce results that go against the spirit of a democratic society." No kidding. You can get elected as president even if you received fewer popular votes than your opponent—it happened with John Quincy Adams, Rutherford B. Hayes and Benjamin Harrison, and the system nearly didn't elect Jimmy Carter in 1976.

Perhaps the most infamous example of breakdown was in 2000 when Americans wound up with George Dubya Bush. One elector of the College actually abstained. (Yep, it's possible—wouldn't you be glad to have that person represent your interests?) Al Gore got more than half-a-million individual popular votes but didn't carry his own home state of Tennessee. Then there was that shady business in Florida, which just happened to be governed at the time by Dubya's brother, Jeb, where the recounts that Al Gore wanted were never finished.

Besides voting for a president, Americans seem to be on an endless escalator of elections, but at least in this case, they're direct elections. The 435 seats in the House of Representatives, plus a third of the 100 Senate seats, are out on the hustings every two years. Imagine having a parliamentary election every two years here with our climate! Good luck with that.

FIRING THE TOP GUY

A PRIME MINISTER IN CANADA may lead, but he's also a hostage to the whims and changing confidence of his Cabinet and caucus, and if your pals turn on you, watch out (Jean Chretien knew he had to skidaddle in 2003 because the end was in sight, and over in Britain, Margaret Thatcher got a stab in the back from her former supporters). But when the top guys want to kick out the PM, it's almost always because they don't want the albatross of an unpopular leader around their necks in the upcoming election.

In the U.S., you'd better like who you elected as president because you're stuck with him for at least four years. Interestingly, the Canadian Parliament website has a section comparing our two systems, and it got its facts wrong, or at least badly phrased: "The only way to get rid of a President before the end of the four-year term is for Congress to impeach and try him or her, which is very hard to do. It has never been done, and has only been three times even attempted." That's not exactly right.

The U.S. Congress in 1868 *did* impeach Andrew Johnson (succeeding on its second attempt) and Bill Clinton in 1999, but the Senate failed to convict either one at their trials. What's actually never been done is a conviction of a president in a Senate trial.

Then there's the case of the odious, corrupt weasel, Richard "Tricky Dick" Nixon. As a congressman, he went around red-baiting and slandering opponents, which is how he got his nickname. As president, he ordered the secret and quite illegal bombing of Cambodia, used his power to try to ruthlessly destroy anyone he considered an enemy, and during the

85

Watergate Crisis, blatantly interfered with independent investigations of the corruption reaching all the way into his office.

Keep in mind he fought to stay. Before he had to face the shame of impeachment, he chose to resign. He was saved thanks to a pardon by his successor, the buffoonish Gerald Ford, a guy who fell out of cars and down airplane gangways, who actually believed the Warren Commission findings and who once said, "If Abe Lincoln were alive today, he'd roll over in his grave."

Nixon lived long enough to see the minor miracle of his reputation improve and the American people forget his crimes.

HOW STUFF GETS DONE:
THEIR WAY VS. OUR WAY

ON PAPER, AT LEAST, THE AMERICAN system looks like you get "checks and balances" that make sure nobody sets himself up as king, and each side of Congress doesn't get too full of itself. The president doesn't introduce the bills he wants—he needs someone in Congress for that. But those in Congress can revise it, add to it, change it or throw it out altogether.

When the House of Representatives passed a health care reform bill in November 2009, you'd think it would have stood out as a historic American liberal victory. But that's mitigated by the fact that the Stupak Amendment was tacked onto the bill as a necessary compromise so the Democrats could win the day; it prevents a woman from using the public funding option to get an abortion, which by the way, is a legal health care procedure in the United States, the same as up here (denying a woman's right to access a medical procedure financially works just as well as denying her through legal means). So under the American system, what you pass into law can wind up as something quite different than what you intended.

With all those convoluted twists and turns for a bill with debated amendments, it's no wonder congressmen have to stay at their job longer during the year than Canadian MPs, which means they may not really be earning significantly more than our guys and gals (see salaries table, page 88). The president can veto a bill, but Congress can overturn his veto with a two-thirds majority. On paper, a president can't declare war, but he's the one who runs the show afterward as commander-in-chief—yet he has to go back to the Senate to get money for it. Certain appointments, like those of Supreme Court judges and ambassadors, have to go through the Senate.

We, on the other hand, have Parliament for all this, with all major bills, like those to spend public funds or raise taxes, originating with the government. Again, we pretty much know what we're getting, because although amendments and changes are made in committee hearings, you don't usually get drastic changes to a bill the way it can happen in the States.

Table: Salaries (2010 Figures)

Canada	US
PM: $315,462 (CAD)	President: $400,000 (USD)
MP: $157,731 (CAD)	Congressman: $175,000 (USD)

(It looks like the Americans earn more, but remember they're on the job more—MPs get almost five months of break!)

Which brings us to what many argue is the major flaw in our system. We have this quaint little holdover from Great Britain, this pensioners' club, which we call a Senate, where you don't need to be elected by the people. If your politics are the right colour in a given year and you have a minimum of $4000 in property, you're in. You're appointed by our Governor General, as chosen by the PM, and you get to stick around until you're 75.

Our Senate has its defenders as a "house of sober second thought," but many Canadians are still wondering what these folks do most days (and if they are, indeed, sober while doing it). Those who think our system is better than the American one can often rationalize to themselves that our Senate rubber-stamps Commons bills and is largely irrelevant.

Then there are the provinces, which have huge powers of their own through their legislatures over certain areas, such as education or labour, except for certain industries. We have regular national arguments about whether the provinces have too much power versus Ottawa, but at least it's a tug o' war among 10 provinces and three territories, not 50 states. Some argue that the PM in our modern age has too much concentrated power, but at the end of the day, we still hold accountable the elected members of his Cabinet—the Justice Minister, the Health Minister and so on—for their individual responsibilities.

Not to be morbid, but when the story emerged of an alleged plot to behead Prime Minister Stephen Harper, as horrific as it was, most Canadians probably scratched their own heads at the legislative pointlessness of such an act. If something happens to a prime minister, his deputy simply takes his place and government rolls along. True, a vice-president can step in for the president, but Americans tend to see their incumbent as almost irreplaceable for his term.

That brings us back to the issue of real power versus power on paper. Jefferson went ahead on his own to make the Louisiana Purchase from Napoleon. Lincoln made himself a dictator and levied troops without consulting Congress, defying the Supreme Court and suspending habeas corpus. Kennedy didn't bother to consult the two Houses about troops sent to Vietnam and outright lied at a news conference when asked in 1962 if Americans were fighting there. Contrary to everything you see in Oliver Stone movies and the myth that he wouldn't have escalated the war, he told friends, "After Cuba, I have to go all the way with this one." Congress certainly didn't know what was going on when Reagan officials made arms sales to Iran and diverted sums to the Nicaraguan Contras. As vice-president, Dick Cheney refused to follow the law and file required documents with the National Archives. Then he tried to get the Archives' security oversight director fired for looking into the matter.

Ironically, in trying to keep the head of their executive branch in check on paper, our neighbours have encouraged a steady evolution in the powers of the president and vice-president so that they can circumvent annoying obstacles like the Constitution and what Congress might do.

It's easy. They simply ignore the Constitution altogether.

The question of who has the better government, Canada or the U.S., is probably less important than to ask, What kind of government do we Canadians want to have? One where our leaders are obligated to account for themselves in an open forum over what they do for us, or one in which the head of government can insist we don't have the right to question his actions because of national security?

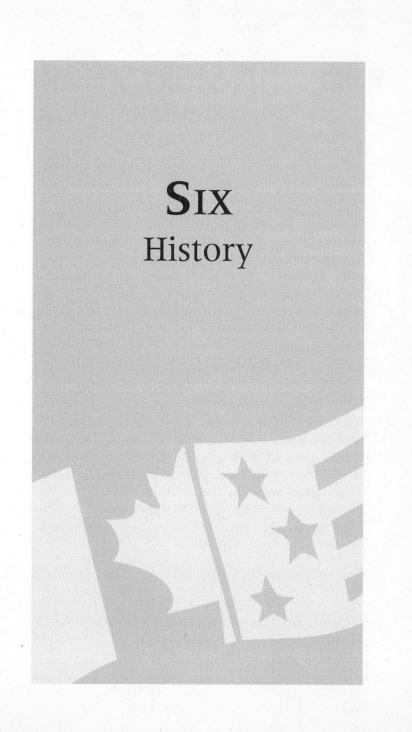

SIX
History

THE STORY SO FAR,
OR WHAT'S PAST IS PIERRE

A GOOD, PASSIONATE ARGUMENT ABOUT who's got the better nation—Canada or the U.S.—really should have some history as ammunition. The problem is that both sides usually go in unarmed.

Those from the United States of Amnesia are raised with the laughable concept that the Founding Fathers all believed in God (who has to be a 'Merican) when many were, truth be known, Deists and agnostics. Americans are also spoon-fed a bunch of myths about heroic battles that often didn't happen the way their textbooks and movies say they did. On our side, we have great compelling history, but somehow the academics hijacked the plot, and a bunch of overworked, uninspired and ignorant teachers have been boring us into narcolepsy ever since 1867.

But fear not! We have some really great episodes in the history of our relations with the U.S. that make us look good. Hell, we even look cool sometimes. But if you're going to approach our history, you'll have to face the fact that America has always been there, and it's not going away any time soon. We have to live with it. And it's best to recognize that we've gone through five stages of grief over this: denial, anger, bargaining, depression and acceptance.

Wipe your eyes, blow your nose—the story gets better, honest.

Denial: America Tries to Invade, Then Goes Home

When the Thirteen Colonies full of wig-wearing, slave-owning gentleman farmers decided to pull off the biggest tax evasion in British history, they got quite anxious about a bunch of Loyalists up here. They never liked the French in Québec, and they especially hated the fact that the guy in charge at that moment, Sir Guy Carleton, worked so hard to protect the rights of the French, like allowing them to practice their own religion and to hold public office (for a bunch of revolutionaries who didn't quite believe in God, like Benjamin Franklin, it was easier to hypocritically pick on Catholicism, which was so foreign and strange compared to good ol' familiar Anglicanism). Carleton's initiative had been one of the revolutionaries' list of "Intolerable Acts" they railed against, even though the Americans were safely hundreds of kilometres away.

Plus they were justifiably a little nervous about the British sticking around upstairs after they had kicked them out on their home ground. The solution? Go invade Québec! They took Montréal easily enough. After patronizing the locals with talk of how this was "a chance for emerging from a humiliating subjection" under British "tyrants," the Americans turned around and banned Christmas Mass. Bad PR move. They soon discovered holding on to Montréal, full of cranky, offended French Canadians, was a pain in the star-spangled ass.

But the real failure came when they tried to take what is now Québec City. The Americans gave that job to their future traitor, Benedict Arnold, a short, arrogant man who already had a big chip on his shoulder over a corruption investigation by Congress. Guy Carleton dismissed him as a "horse jockey." Arnold didn't think much of Carleton either, expecting he'd have his British opponent flying a white flag within a month. The trouble was that the American general didn't know how to read a map, or perhaps he just couldn't get his hands on a decent one. What he thought was 290 kilometres to Québec from Massachusetts was 560 kilometres! And Arnold's men had to cross that distance through icy snowfalls, discouraging floods and let's not forget the punishing wilderness. Within weeks, his soldiers were chowing down on their own shoe leather.

Arnold did finally make it—with only half his army. He got reinforcements when General Richard Montgomery brought men up from Montréal. That didn't phase Carleton. He'd served as quartermaster under James Wolfe during the Battle of the Plains of Abraham in 1759, and he knew exactly the kind of pounding the walls of Québec could take (keep in mind, Wolfe's army never actually got within those walls during the battle). So when Montgomery sent him a letter demanding surrender and no doubt promising he'd huff and he'd puff, Carleton tossed it into a fire without even reading it.

In the early hours of December 31, 1775, the Americans made a two-pronged attack on Québec—right in the middle of a blizzard. Montgomery was shot in the head, and his men essentially decided, "To hell with this" and left their dead officers in the snow. As for Arnold, he was carried away from the attack after getting shot in the leg. When it was all over, roughly 400 Americans were captured (and probably grateful for it after fighting in whiteout conditions), while 60 more were killed or wounded.

The Americans decided to stick around until spring, but their timing was still off. By May, British ships were sailing up the St. Lawrence with fresh troops, and the Americans slunk away and decided it would be much better if they stuck to defending what they already had instead of trying to take more. With Loyalists escaping to Halifax and parts of Québec, and the Americans deciding to leave Canada alone after the fiasco under Arnold, the two sides decided to ignore each other. For a while.

Anger: America Will Invade and Get It Right This Time, Damn It! (Nope)

There are so many fun things about our side in the War of 1812 that it's a pity it's not taught better in Canadian classrooms and that we don't have a national holiday to rub it in. The burning of the White House is a great tale, but there's so much more. Just as the Americans singing about the "rockets' red glare" in their national anthem is about fighting us, we did so well that every so often, we should switch the words to "O Canada" so we can sing, "Nyah-Nyah, Ny-Nyaaaah...."

By the way, putting the war under the heading of "anger" is quite accurate. The British got mad because the United States decided to impose a kind of "self embargo" of its territorial waters, what with the tit-for-tat blockades of ports going on in the War of 1812 with Napoleon. Napoleon was the one everyone should have blamed, but Washington chose to focus on British "outrages." Meanwhile, the British Royal Navy had become something like a power-mad highway cop on the high seas, blaring his siren and barking through the bullhorn to "pull over." Its ships grabbed merchant seamen and fishermen and forced them to join its ranks whenever it needed them.

On top of all that, the Americans claimed that the British were stirring up the Natives on frontier settlements. The truth is that the First Nations hardly needed anyone to stir them up, since the Americans kept encroaching on their territory by the Ohio River.

War was perhaps inevitable—and the Americans were thrilled to have it, confident they would win. The Republican Speaker of the House of Representatives and one of the biggest warmongers in Congress, Henry Clay boasted all that was needed to take Canada was the Kentucky militia. Thomas Jefferson, who should have remembered what happened to Benedict Arnold, sneered, "The acquisition of Canada this year, as far as the neighbourhood of Québec, will be a mere matter of marching." Hey, Tommy, remember how well your guys marched last time? But truthfully, the odds weren't in our favour. Fewer than 6000 regular soldiers were available for the fight, and a pitiful 1200 of those were spread thin across the garrisons of Upper Canada.

We did, however, have Isaac Brock.

Isaac Brock: Canada's first military badass

One day, someone will get smart at Alliance Atlantis or another film company and make a movie of this guy, because he sure deserves one. Born in Guernsey in Britain's quiet Channel Islands, young Isaac was a gentle, bookish boy who was a talented athlete— swimming, boxing, fencing, he could do them all. When he was a young officer stationed in Barbados, nobody in his regiment thought you could get a horse up the limestone ledges of Mount Hillaby, which is 340 metres high. Brock did it, always believing, "The word 'impossible' should not be found in a soldier's dictionary."

A bully once made the bad decision to challenge him to a duel. Brock was more than six feet tall and would have made a big pistol target. But he quickly accepted on one condition—he and his opponent had to shoot across the width of a handkerchief. That meant point-blank range! Not surprisingly, the bully backed down, and he quit the regiment some time later.

While Brock was disappointed to be sent to a backwater like Canada, he would soon get all the action he would ever want. Even before war was officially declared, he was chomping at the bit, urging his superior to let him go conduct some pre-emptive strikes. This was shrewd. The Americans were sending men north and mobilizing them so that they'd be ready when the "formal" word was given. Lucky for us, the Americans faced Brock— and they sent a complete idiot.

This was Brigadier General William Hull, a revolutionary hero well past his prime at 60, who dragged his heels and took weeks to obey an order to take his army across the Detroit River. Because his soldiers had to plod through rain and mud in an area called Black Swamp, he chartered a schooner to carry sick men, his officers' baggage, his musicians and his own personal papers up Lake Erie to Fort Detroit. When he learned the war was on, he panicked and tried to overtake the ship—which was strange, since he knew ahead of time that Washington was about to declare war. It was, after all, the whole point of why he'd come up in the first place. Brock heard about the schooner and sent word off, and soon redcoats in a longboat captured the ship. Since Hull had been foolish enough to include his plans and papers, Major General Isaac Brock now knew exactly how many of the enemy were coming and where they would be. The British officer in charge of the capture operation made Hull's musicians play "God Save the King."

Hull invaded anyway, bringing his army to what is now Windsor. In the meantime, Brock had been reading all those captured dispatches and papers, getting insight into his enemy. This Hull, it turned out, was scared witless (well, he was already witless, but we'll keep it clean) of "savages" and a possible Native massacre. Brock, on the other hand, was a fast pal with Native warrior Tecumseh, and he genuinely respected the First Nations. He sent Hull a note and played on his fear like a grand piano. He demanded Hull's surrender and, like the "good cop" in an interrogation room, basically warned the American General in so many words, "Hey, look buddy, you know I can be reasonable, but when the battle starts, well...I won't be able to hold these guys back."

Tecumseh was in on the joke. He had his men walk in a circle three times past the fort to make his numbers look larger, while Brock's militia dressed up in old redcoat uniforms to make them look more impressive. Just as the battle got underway, Hull put up the white flag and asked for a three-day respite. Three days? Brock's reply was he would give them three hours, or he "would blow up every one of them."

Meet the first genuine Canadian Forces badass. When Brock eventually lost his life in the Battle of Queenston

Heights, the Americans fired their own guns at Fort Niagara in tribute.

Brock wasn't the only hero for Canada in the war. We had them both on land and at sea. Captain Philip Broke of the *Shannon* was the type of commander who believed in drill, then more drill, to be followed by drill. When his ship was to be sent into battle, he was determined to be ready. His gun crew practiced with live ammunition, and he paid for new gun sights and other aiming devices out of his own pocket. As the *Shannon* sailed into Boston Harbor, he sent a note to the commander of the much larger American vessel, the famous *Chesapeake*, to "try the fortunes of our respective flags." If this were film, the subtitles for the British would read: "I say, old man, after you've finished your claret, could you please sail out so I can blow your head off with a cannonball? Brilliant, much obliged."

But Captain James Lawrence of the *Chesapeake* was already on his way. Both vessels had 38 guns. Lawrence's ship was larger, but he didn't have much faith in his inexperienced crew and had already dashed off a letter in his cabin that asked a friend to look after his family. All of Broke's insistence on training paid off. The Shannon blasted holes in the *Chesapeake*, and the two ships collided. Broke's men jumped aboard the enemy decks, flashing their cutlasses and firing their muskets.

Lawrence, mortally wounded by sniper fire, saw his ship being boarded and shouted, "Don't give up the ship! Don't give up the ship!" Later, this line would be used to style him as a hero. Except his men *did* give up the ship after 15 minutes of fighting, while he lay dying in his cabin. As for Broke, he got a bad cutlass wound to the head, but he lived to see himself being cheered in Halifax as the *Chesapeake* was towed into the harbour. American tourists will no doubt thank you for being so helpful when they visit the city's Maritime Museum of the Atlantic and you point out that artifacts of their captured ship are on display.

Most of our boasts about the war are usually that "we burned down the White House." That's not quite true, and in fact, the real story is much, much better.

The Americans had come up and burned York, looting homes and beating up civilians, and some British criminals let out of prison helped with the rampage. York had fewer than 1000 residents, so hitting back at the national capital of Washington was bound to have a more powerful impact. And our side hit back hard. Twenty Royal Navy warships sailed into Chesapeake Bay, scaring the life out of the Americans, who didn't know where the ships would make landfall. The American Secretary of War, John Armstrong, guessed wrong—he thought Baltimore made more strategic sense, so he left Washington pretty much unfortified.

Still, there were 7000 Americans facing 4000 British troops when the attack started on a sticky, hot day with a high of 40°C. While President James Madison and members of his Cabinet watched on horseback, sweating through their suit jackets, the generals bickered over who outranked who to order defensive positions. The British fired off rockets, and American militiamen ran for their lives. "Never did men with arms in their hands make better use of their legs," joked one British officer.

Madison raced back to the White House to find his dinner on the table and that his wife had left in a wagon packed with velvet curtains, silverware, boxes of papers and a portrait of George Washington cut out of its frame. Today, Dolly Madison's hasty packing and running away is considered "heroic" in American textbooks. As for President Madison, he got on a horse and rode to safety in Virginia.

Back in Washington, the British were far more restrained than the Americans had been at York. Contrary to popular legend, the White House didn't get its name because we burned it, and they slapped on a quick coat of white paint—that's a myth. What the British soldiers *did* do was help themselves to the presidential booze, try on some shirts since theirs were getting all sweaty what with invading and all, and cram their pockets full of souvenirs before they set fire to the curtains and furniture and gutted the joint.

But the British only picked on government buildings— the White House, the Capitol, the Treasury. At around midnight after the battle, a couple of women begged Rear Admiral George Cockburn not to torch the offices of the government paper, *The National Intelligencer*. Cockburn had been annoyed by the way the paper had portrayed him as a villain, but just the same, he had his men take the office contents into the street to burn in a bonfire. When another group of women strolled by, unaccompanied, Cockburn purred, "Now did you expect to see me such a clever fellow? Were you not prepared to see a savage, ferocious creature, such as [the editor] represented me? But you see I am quite harmless; don't be afraid, I will take better care of you than [Madison] did!"

As the fires burned down, refreshments were brought out, and Cockburn and his officers continued trying to chat up the American women. When the British finally quit Washington and sailed out of Maryland, they took away 200 captured guns and thousands of musket cartridges. Remembering the humiliating sprint of Americans off the field, the British took to calling the battle for Washington "The Bladensburg Races."

So there you are. Our guys invaded the capital, drank the Americans' liquor and got an opportunity to sweet talk the Americans' women. Now isn't that better than just burning the White House?

Bargaining: Squabbles, Schemes and Deals

The truth is we had free trade before we even had Confederation. A reciprocity treaty had been signed in 1854, but the Americans tore it up by 1866 as a way to keep American farmers competitive in the aftermath of the Civil War. Not that any deal made us trust each other more. The whole reason our country extended west in the first place was because our drunk of a grand states-man, John A. Macdonald, didn't want it falling into American hands: "I would be quite willing to leave that whole country a wilderness for the next half century, but I fear that if Englishmen do not go there, Yankees will!"

He was right. Washington's Secretary of State, W.H. Seward, a Machiavellian who loved to insult Englishmen and who tried for a while to get rid of his own former boss, Lincoln, admitted to Congress that he took Alaska off Russia's hands in 1867 because he coveted British Columbia.

It was free trade that ultimately brought down one of our most successful prime ministers, Wilfred Laurier. After trying to get us our own navy and being blasted for it by both the French and the English, Laurier pinned his political hopes on a new reciprocity treaty. It was a bad call. Tory leader Robert Borden demanded to know, "Should we, at the time of our greatest successes and realizations, lose hope and abandon the battle for our national existence?"

Stephen Leacock hated the idea. So did Rudyard Kipling, who suggested Canada was risking its own soul. It didn't help that American politicians rubbed their palms together with delight, both in secret and out in the open, oblivious to the nuances of Canadian politics. President William Taft wrote in a private letter to Teddy Roosevelt that the new deal would create "a current of business between Western Canada and the United States that would make Canada only an adjunct of the United States." The letter was leaked.

Meanwhile, the Speaker of the House of Representatives, Champ Clark, beamed, "I have no doubt whatever that the day is not far distant when Great Britain will joyfully see all her North American possessions become part of this Republic." He casually added later, "We are preparing to annex Canada."

Up in Ottawa, Laurier must have been hanging his head, thinking: "Oh, *greeeeaaaat*, thanks a lot." By the fall of 1911, he and his Liberals were voted out, and Robert Borden was in power.

But Canadians have never had their chance to comment, let alone vote, on all of our dealings with our neighbour. In 1940, Mackenzie King signed a joint defence agreement with Franklin Roosevelt in the president's private train car near Ogdensburg, New York. We wouldn't know what we got ourselves into until after World War Two was over.

We didn't get screwed all the time—at times it seems the Americans simply weren't paying close attention. Lyndon Johnson didn't bother to learn Lester Pearson's first name before he announced the Auto Pact in 1965, calling him "Drew" in front of reporters. Pearson and Johnson had met at the president's Texas ranch, dining on catfish and steak, and then the next morning they signed a deal that ensured the U.S. big car companies would manufacture a substantial portion of their production lines at Canadian factories.

In the early years, the Auto Pact was considered a major victory for our economy. But of course it meant we never developed a car industry of our own, and as the Pact was gradually superseded by free trade deals, evolving economics, labour disputes as well as changing political regimes, we've grown to worry about layoffs at the factories in Windsor when someone gets the jitters in Detroit. But those lessons were ones to be debated in the future.

Nobody saw it coming, but our relationship with the U.S. was about to be rocked in a big way.

Depression: I Still Love You, but I Think It's Time We See Other Exports

After Pierre Trudeau was swept into power in 1968, Richard Nixon moved into the Oval Office. Our PM was "that asshole Trudeau" to Tricky Dick. An episode up in the Arctic helped make our relations with the U.S. frostier.

An oil company tanker, the S.S. *Manhattan*, decided it would traipse its way through the Northwest Passage like a drunken merchant marine sailor, and just like your average annoying drunk, it needed help finding its way— from Canadian icebreakers. Ottawa didn't take kindly to a tanker meandering through our waters, which the U.S. has always blithely declared are "international" (until someone wanders into theirs), or that these ships proved—and still prove—to regularly cause ecological disasters by breaking up. The Trudeau government passed the Arctic Waters Pollution Prevention Bill in 1970, declaring it would assert control over all commercial shipping in the North. And just so America got the message, it announced it would refuse to accept the jurisdiction of the International Court of Justice on this one. Imagine! Canada saying it wouldn't listen to the Hague!

So first we took *Manhattan*—to task, that is. The next time the vessel wanted to make a try through the passage, it had to meet our safety standards.

It was early in Trudeau's first term when he made his famous observation in a speech to the U.S. National Press Club that living next to the U.S. "is like sleeping next to an elephant." He was right, and commentators and writers have been pounding the metaphorical elephant into a dead horse ever since. More interesting—and awfully familiar—is how Nixon told the world in 1971 that he had to control the rampant deficit and fight inflation, so there would be "no more Uncle Sugar." He floated the U.S. dollar and slapped a 10 percent surtax on most imports.

The duties on our goods were bad enough, but it could have been worse. Former Governor of Texas turned Treasury Secretary John Connally, who could be a pugnacious jerk (he was a hawk on Vietnam and once told Europeans the U.S. dollar was "our currency, but your problem"), was hell bent on scrapping the Auto Pact. It was only thanks to cooler and more informed heads at the State Department that he didn't get his way.

As it was, things got ugly when Deputy Finance Minister Simon Reisman—no slouch when it came to shouting matches—came to Washington to meet with Connally. Connally started to read a brief meant for Japan, and Reisman didn't hesitate to correct him on his facts. The Treasury Secretary refused to exempt Canada, which put $300 million worth of exports and thousands of jobs at risk. The story goes that when the meeting was over, our pit bull of a deputy minister stubbed out his cigar on the Texan's desk.

The issue would have to be settled—or not—by bigger heads, so Trudeau flew down to Washington to meet

Nixon. The talk between the two leaders was civil enough (Trudeau later called Nixon "very strange"), but made little progress. If Washington was prepared to treat its neighbour this way, warned Trudeau, Canada could always reply in kind and tax snowbirds who pumped half-a-billion dollars each year into the Florida economy.

When Nixon visited Ottawa in 1972 the surcharge on our goods had been lifted, but his analysis of our relations amounted to a eulogy: "It is time for us to recognize that we have very separate identities; that we have significant differences; and that nobody's interest are furthered when these realities are obscured." Translation: it's not me, darling, it's you. "Each nation," Nixon told the joint session of Parliament, "must determine the path of its own progress."

It was a depressing state of affairs. Trudeau's government tried to build trade with Japan and Europe—with so-so results. Sure, they loved our raw materials. Our manufactured goods? Not so much. One of the Liberals' success stories, however, was the creation of Petro-Canada in 1975, which would develop the Alberta tar sands and tag an export surcharge on every barrel going to the U.S. That ticked off the U.S., which didn't like those Socialist Canadians gouging an ally (hmmm, how quickly they forget). But Washington soon calmed down, since it still got its natural gas from the north with no headaches.

The surcharge also annoyed Alberta's Tory premier Peter Lougheed, and ever since the seventies, Albertans occasionally let out the battle cry, "Let the eastern bastards freeze in the dark." While the Liberals and Conservatives made Petro-Canada into a political football over the years, it slowly became a nationalist symbol of economic pride as it evolved from Crown Corporation to its shaky privatization to its recent merger with Suncor. And we're still sending oil to the States, a lot of it (see page 74).

Mutual grumbling over a laundry list of economic and political issues continued. The Americans didn't like how Trudeau got chummy with Cuba's Fidel Castro (Castro would be an honorary pallbearer at Trudeau's funeral in 2000). In 1977, Canada declared a 200-mile territorial limit to guard our fisheries, which we're still squabbling over. In 1981, Americans had a former actor as president, Ronald Reagan, who quoted movie dialogue as if it were historical truth. (He once told an audience how one airman told another in a flaming bomber in World War Two, "It's okay—we'll go down together." Besides the clear idiocy of these words being impossible to be recounted, they came from a movie.) Our philosopher-king, Trudeau, had become a lion in winter, hated by many at home for his past sins with the economy but still respected on the world stage—especially when he talked peace while Reagan banged Cold War drums. One of the Pentagon brain trust, irritated by our PM's efforts, groaned, "Oh, God, Trudeau's at it again."

He wouldn't be at it much longer, and the Americans would soon have somebody they preferred dealing with.

Acceptance: When a Tree Falls, That Sound Is Surcharges

Our prime minister for most of the eighties, Brian Mulroney didn't talk about elephants—he told the Economic Club in New York in 1984, "Canada is open for business again." Mulroney received more than polite acceptance from America's President Reagan. They were pals, crooning "When Irish Eyes Are Smiling" together at the Shamrock Summit in Québec City in 1984. Then Mulroney negotiated the controversial Free Trade Agreement, which was intended to phase out all tariffs between the two countries by 1998—and yet somehow allowed the U.S. to keep slapping surcharges on our softwood lumber.

Even with many Canadians growing to dislike Mulroney and wanting him gone as the 1990s got rolling, we still wound up with the North American Free Trade Agreement (NAFTA). We keep debating that one...and our softwood lumber. NAFTA certainly isn't the last word on our economic squabbles (see page 49).

The pivotal moment of 9/11 simultaneously brought us closer together with the United States and pushed us apart. We weren't recognized for our efforts to help in the wake of the attack (see page 248), nor have we been granted our due over our contribution to fighting the common enemy of terrorism (see page 160). Yet while Fox News blathers on about us being either a wimp or a threat (it can't seem to make up its mind), Barack Obama chose Canada as his first foreign country to visit after he was elected president.

"I love this country and think that we could not have a better friend and ally," said Obama. "And so I'm going to do everything that I can to make sure that our relationship is strengthened."

We'll see what happens.

QUICK! WE'LL GET
THEM WHILE THEIR BACKS ARE
TURNED!

THERE'S A FUNNY POSTSCRIPT OF paranoia to our gradually stabilizing relationship. Both America and Canada drew up plans to invade each other—only a few years after they fought side-by-side against those pesky Huns.

After the Great War, the supposed "war to end all wars," it was reasonable to expect the only military threat to ever come again to Canada would be from... yep, the south. What to do? Well, as soon as we knew for sure they were coming, we'd hit them first!

Canada's plan for invasion was called Defence Scheme No. 1. It was the brainchild of Canada's director of military operations and intelligence, Colonel James Sutherland "Buster" Brown. In 1921, Brown got permission to drive undercover with four lieutenant-colonels, all in civilian clothes, to do reconnaissance in states like Vermont and northern New York. It's hard to resist Pierre Berton's characterization of the plan as "madcap"—especially when this Buster Brown and his officers, as Berton writes in *Marching As To War*, were picking up gas station maps, chatting with locals and "tooling along the gravel roads, snapping their Kodaks at bridges and everything else from canal locks to highway overpasses...."

Brown's plan didn't rely on us winning, mind you. Oh, no. After we invaded and captured key spots like Seattle, Minneapolis and Albany, we were supposed to hold out and wait for Mother England to show up! "His plan was to start sending people south quickly because surprise would be more important than preparation," according to Floyd Rudmin, a Canadian psychology professor who wrote about the war plan in his book, *Bordering on Aggression*. "At a certain point, he figured they'd be stopped and then retreat, blowing up bridges and tearing up railroad tracks to slow the Americans down."

Brown had what can only be charitably described as a "loose" style when it came to writing up intelligence data. About the people of Vermont, he believed, "If they are not actually lazy, they have a very deliberate way of working and apparently believe in frequent rests and gossip. The women throughout the rural districts appear to be a heavy and not very comely lot." Hey, if you're going to invade a nation, better go find the babes.

By 1928, however, the Canadian Forces had a new chief of the general staff, one who expected Britain, Canada and the U.S. to get along, and most of the documents for Defence Scheme No. 1 were burned and forgotten. It wasn't until 1974 that a Canadian historian, Robert Preston, dug up the raw reports once again and learned what Brown had been up to.

Meanwhile, the Americans had also been looking over their shoulders all this time. In the late 1920s, they imagined a war with Britain sparking over international trade. They assumed Canada would be used as a launch point for invasion, with British and Canadian troops attacking Buffalo, Detroit and Albany (turns out they were right on that one). To counter this, the Americans came up with a "Joint Army and Navy Basic War Plan—Red," which has become popularly known as War Plan Red.

They planned to first capture Halifax, robbing Britain of its key Canadian port, then go after power plants at Niagara Falls. The U.S. Army would march on three fronts, including an attempt from Vermont to capture Montréal and Québec City (they never learn).

The Americans didn't forsee much trouble in seizing Winnipeg's rail system through an offensive from Grand Forks (conveniently forgetting that in the prairie landscape of southern Manitoba, the Winnipeggers would see the Yanks coming with time to spare, especially since every year if you drive your car past the perimeter, you can see snowstorms from kilometres away). In 1935, the plan incorporated the new idea of building three military airfields near the Canadian border and disguising them as civilian airports. Brilliant! We'd *never* notice those as we drove into North Dakota! We'd never look up, after all, and see clearly non-commercial aircraft taking off! The goal was "ULTIMATELY TO GAIN COMPLETE CONTROL." (The planners liked capitals a lot).

War Plan Red was formally drawn up and approved by the War Department in 1930 then updated in 1934 and 1935. Its creators expected it would be a "long duration" struggle because the "RED race," i.e. British, is "more or less phlegmatic" but "noted for its ability to fight to a finish." According to the plan, those menacing Brits might also reinforce their numbers with "coloured" troops from their colonies: "Some of the coloured races, however, come of good fighting stock, and, under white leadership, can be made into very efficient troops."

Yes, we noticed. They were particularly good at fighting after they wanted to move here and leave the southern states, the ones where they were being used as farm implements. We noticed what efficient troops they were when they joined up as Loyalists and were kicking your revolutionary ass.

Unfortunately for the Americans who stamped SECRET on War Plan Red's cover, two generals testified in a closed-door session of the House Military Affairs Committee, and someone published the details by mistake. Ottawa stamped its foot in outrage, forgetting it had burned its own plan only a little while ago, and the whole mess made it onto the front page of the *New York Times* in May 1935. When Ottawa protested, Franklin Roosevelt said of course, we're not planning to invade you! We're friends! Buddy! Pal! Then in the summer, the U.S. Army held the biggest war games in its history—with 36,500 soldiers—up in the farmland of upstate New York (it's now the military's training site, Fort Drum). But don't worry, Canucks.

All this time, of course, while Americans and Canadians were drawing up their daffy plans, Mussolini stole power with his Fascists in Italy, Hitler arranged the Reichstag to burn down in Berlin and took over in Germany, and militarists were triumphant in Japan.

On the score of getting our priorities wrong, you might say it's a tie.

(ANTI-) AMERICAN HISTORY: FUN AND DISTURBING THINGS AMERICANS DON'T KNOW BUT SHOULD, AND THAT YOU CAN SELF-RIGHTEOUSLY BEAT THEM OVER THE HEAD WITH

ONE OF OUR FATHERS OF CONFEDERATION, D'Arcy McGee warned us early on about eagles looking our way. McGee argued the United States was ever hungry "for the acquisition of new territory, and the inexorable law of democratic existence seems to be its absorption. They coveted Florida and seized it; they coveted Louisiana and purchased it; they coveted Texas and stole it; and then they picked a quarrel with Mexico, which ended by their getting California."

All of which happens to be true. Imagine what McGee would have thought if he knew even more damning facts. He was, after all, an Irish nationalist who denounced the Fenians—the lunatic fringe terrorists who thought the best way to free Ireland from British control was to ride up from the U.S. to attack Canada (yep, really). President Andrew Johnson actually sympathized with them and chose to do nothing to stop these regular small invasions. And Johnson wished he could have done more to help! We know this because Britain had a spy, one Thomas Beach, who managed to penetrate into the inner circles of the IRA and right into the Oval Office. Fortunately, the Canadian militia was quite skilled at kicking the Fenians out of our country.

So here are some other interesting highlights every self-righteous patriotic Canadian should know about

113

America's international adventurism, which goes right back to its revolutionary days.

- Ten years after the Declaration of Independence—which says whenever a form of government becomes destructive, it's the right of the people to abolish it, blah, blah, blah—a group of newly-minted Americans in Massachusetts realized they were paying more in taxes to the infant regime than to the British. Washington and the other great landowners were horrified that they were expected to live up to their word. Worse, the discontent was apparently growing as well in Rhode Island. They quickly put down the rebellion led by Captain Daniel Shays and then rushed to rewrite their hallowed documents, making sure "to take into consideration the Trade and Commerce of the United States."

- The brilliantly talented Renaissance man, slave-owner and hypocrite, Thomas Jefferson defended the Reign of Terror of the French Revolution, thinking it was worth it. That's right, the hero of American democracy backed the terrorists!

- One of America's Founding Fathers and co-author of *The Federalist Papers*, Alexander Hamilton was "Agent Number Seven," a spy for the British. The vice-president under Jefferson, Aaron Burr, was a spy for the Directory of France, and a later commander of the U.S. army, James Wilkinson, acted as a spy for Spain.

- William Henry Harrison, before becoming one of the shortest-term presidents ever (he droned on for almost two hours at his inaugural address in rainy weather, then died from a cold after 30 days in office), liked to get Native chiefs drunk so he could take advantage of them in treaty negotiations and also repealed Indiana's prohibition of slavery.

- As assistant secretary of the Navy, Teddy Roosevelt ordered the U.S. fleet to the Philippines while the government was in recess in 1898 and helped orchestrate America's war with Spain. The U.S. first promised revolutionaries it would recognize Filipino independence, then negotiated Spain's surrender behind their backs and fought a war with the Filipinos so it could annex their islands.

- In 1945, after World War Two, the Americans installed a military governor in Korea, General John R. Hodge—without bothering to ask the Koreans, mind you—who put Japanese colonial administrators back in office until the locals got angry. The anti-Communist strongman that America later backed as South Korea's president, Syngman Rhee, arranged massacres, had bridges cut on the Han River that prevented thousands from escaping Communist rule, and embezzled more than $20 million before he fled the country on a CIA jet. Despite all this, Canada and other nations still helped the U.S. fight the Korean War (see page 154).

- As External Affairs Minister, Lester Pearson had wanted the Korean War solved diplomatically and scolded Harry Truman's Secretary of State, Dean Acheson, recommending the U.S. ought to "take more notice of what we do and what we say." From Washington, Acheson wrote back, "If you think that after the agonies we have gone through here to get agreement on this matter, we're going to start all over with our NATO allies, especially you moralistic, interfering Canadians, then you're crazy." And we know how well Korea worked out for everybody.

- The U.S. was part of the international alliance that helped put down China's Boxer Rebellion, which was about trying to get foreigners out and stop meddling in their country.

- In the 1900s, the U.S. backed dictatorial regimes in Nicaragua (where it later installed the ruling Somoza family) and other parts of Central America. It's not just lefties saying this—one of their own generals, the highly decorated Smedley Butler, admitted it in a change-of-heart book, *War Is a Racket*. He wrote, "I helped make Haiti and Cuba a decent place for the National City Bank boys to collect revenues in. I helped in the raping of half a dozen Central American republics for the benefit of Wall Street...I brought light to the Dominican Republic for the American sugar interests in 1916. I helped make Honduras right for the American fruit companies in 1903."

- In the 1950s, Iraq was one of those important "buffer" states the U.S. liked to keep on its side against the Soviet Union. But in 1958, a general named Abdul Karim Qassim overthrew the country's monarchy, pulled out of the security alliance known as the Baghdad Pact and bought weapons from Moscow. Washington couldn't have that, so they hired a clever young fellow to be part of a six-man hit squad. An American official who knew him back then called him a "cutthroat" and a "thug" who had no class.

By the way, this Iraqi cutthroat's name was Saddam Hussein.

In 1959, Saddam—who would later have thousands of Iraqi Kurds slaughtered—wasn't skilled at murdering people yet, and instead of killing Qassim, only wounded him and was wounded himself by one of the other killers' bullets. An American spymaster said the whole op "bordered on farce." (One of Saddam's team had a hand grenade that got stuck in his coat.) Saddam fled to Cairo, where the CIA looked after him. Qassim wound up being assassinated by someone else anyway, in a fresh coup in 1963—which came as a complete surprise to the Americans. No matter. The CIA and Saddam Hussein found each other useful later in 1980 when the Agency fed him intelligence in the Iran-Iraq War.

Other Nasty Things the U.S. Did

Under John F. Kennedy, encouraged the *coup d'etat* that overthrew South Vietnam's President Ngo Dinh Diem

Through the CIA, orchestrated a *coup d'etat* to have Iran's elected prime minister, Mohammed Mosaddeq, overthrown in 1953 so the Shah of Iran could rule autocratically with the help of the sinister intelligence service SAVAK, set up with the help of the CIA

Supplied thousands of gallons of napalm to the right-wing side during the Greek Civil War in 1948 to dump on leftist partisans. It later supported the colonels who seized power in Greece and who established the rule of a right-wing junta from 1967 to 1974. To his credit, the U.S. ambassador to Greece called the takeover a "rape of democracy." The CIA's chief of station in Athens snapped, "How can you rape a whore?" After anti-American protests in 1999, President Bill Clinton expressed regret for the role of the U.S. in the coup

Is suspected of helping the coup that ousted the democratically elected Marxist president of Chile, Salvador Allende, so it could install General Pinochet

Because too many people in the U.S. get their history through movies instead of reading nifty books like this one (alas, so do we), you can always stroll with your

American sparring partner from the bar to Blockbusters and pick up the following DVDs:

Bury My Heart at Wounded Knee (treatment of Native Americans)

Reds (the completely forgotten history of Socialist and labour activism in the U.S.)

Missing (Chile)

Z (Greece)

The Killing Fields (Cambodia)

Salvador (El Salvador)

Traitor (the War on Terror)

The Battle of Algiers (Okay, this last one's not about the U.S., it's about France's desperate effort to hang on to Algeria, but boy, does it ever explain Iraq and Afghanistan for you; the Pentagon had a screening of it.)

IMPERIALIST CANADA:
MAHDI, BOERS AND TURKS
(THE CARIBBEAN KIND)

CANADIANS LOVE TO POINT OUT examples of American international aggression like the ones in the last section. We also sometimes pat ourselves on the back for our justified and comfortingly liberal guilt over our treatment of indigenous peoples, our treatment of black people (Africville in Halifax, for example, was a poverty-stricken nightmare in which the authorities offered no services, then charged the residents taxes) and our treatment of Asian people (the Chinese head tax, the Japanese internments).

Although some of us bash Americans for imperialism, we've also been imperialistic ourselves a few times. Fortunately, we redress these things better.

From Winnipeg to Khartoum

When the fabled megalomaniac Charles "Chinese" Gordon chose to defend Khartoum in 1884 (even though he had the option to leave and Britain had already decided to quit the place), Canadians were ready to rescue him and his Egyptian soldiers. John A. Macdonald was reluctant to involve Canada in an imperial fight, but he couldn't really object when it would be mostly civilians signing up. Britain's man to fetch Gordon was General Garnet Wolseley, the same Wolseley who commanded the Red River Expedition to deal with Louis Riel. He wanted to hire 300 voyageurs to steer boats down the Nile to go deal with Sudan's infamous leader, the Mahdi. Now there's a picture!

Canadian voyageurs in Ottawa in 1884 before the Nile Expedition

By this time, of course, there weren't really any voyageurs left. No matter—French Canadian log rafters would do. Officers from units like the Winnipeg Rifles and the Governor General's Foot Guards were recruited, and an ad went into the *Manitoba Daily Free Press* for 50 "good boatmen." What the expedition got was a bunch of Winnipeg office types, including lawyers, who had no boating experience but who wanted thrills. (British newspapers later dismissed these guys as "photographers, cooks, bank cashiers...all out for a holiday.") By the time the expedition was ready to leave Canada, there were 360 recruits, many from around Ottawa, Trois-Rivières and Caughnawaga, Québec and Manitoba—all headed for exotic Africa on a rescue mission.

They reached Alexandria by early October 1884, which was almost 2580 kilometres downriver from Khartoum. From the depot of Wadi Halfa, the boatmen were expected to carry, row and sail 800 modified Royal Navy whaling vessels nine metres long and almost two metres wide, while accompanying a dozen British soldiers and their supplies for almost a third of a year. Later, a British sergeant would claim, "Nothing less than the levelheadedness and surpassing skills of the voyageurs could have guided us. Many were the hairbreadth escapes from death...."

Unfortunately, the rescue op was a bit of a bust. Typhoid killed several of the Canadians, and the six-month contract ended for others, who wanted to go home. Those that chose to leave got a hero's welcome from citizens when they reached Ottawa on the return leg in February 1885, some wearing Turkish and Egyptian clothing and loaded with souvenirs like shields and cockatoos. Meanwhile, back in Sudan, the remaining voyageurs had to navigate their boats away from the crocodile-infested banks of the Nile, all while Wolseley tried to save Khartoum from falling.

Too late

The Mahdi knew the British were coming, so he stepped up taking Khartoum. Gordon—depicted as a hero later in everything from paintings to a Charlton Heston movie—was beheaded and his body was thrown down a well. The only battle for the Canadians happened at a spot called Kirbekan when British soldiers launched an attack against the Mahdi's dervishes. One Canadian officer, Frederick Denison, took part and was later decorated by Queen Victoria. The boatmen were less gallant—when the smoke of the rifles cleared, they looted bodies for guns, knives and swords.

"Such was the effect of Gordon's death that across the empire, and even in the United States, young men volunteered to go to Sudan to avenge him," writes Peter Pigott in his fascinating *Canada in Sudan*. The Governor General was bombarded with pleas from across Canada

121

to set up an expedition to go avenge Gordon. Our future Minister for the Militia in the Great War and all-around loon, Sam Hughes wanted a unit sent right away (Hughes later dashed off to the Boer War, where he irritated the British command so much as a supply officer that they forbade him at one point to wear a uniform). Macdonald still wouldn't have it. He made it clear: if you go, you don't go as part of Canada's armed forces. "Our men and money," he wrote to Charles Tupper, "would...be sacrificed to get [Prime Minister William] Gladstone and Co. out of a hole they have plunged themselves into by their own imbecility."

More than 120 years later, Canada is in Sudan, working for the Sudanese. Since January 2006, Canada has provided more than $163 million in humanitarian aid to war-affected civilians. Our military presence—through UN peacekeeping operations and the African Union–UN Hybrid Operation in Darfur—has tried to keep the fragile nation from completely imploding. Surprisingly, we have more military personnel there than the U.S. does (see page 149).

The Boer War: Four Against Fifty

Canada was also involved in the Boer War—well, the country's English volunteers were. Its French citizens wanted nothing to do with it (those wise French). More than 8000 Canadians enlisted to defend the Empire in South Africa, and we even had our own heroic exploits to excite newspaper readers back home. For instance, at Leliefontein on November 7, 1900, three Canadians won the Victoria Cross for keeping an artillery gun out of enemy hands. Four Canadians held off 50 Boers in another episode. The war gets less heroic, though, when you remember the British invented the concentration camp in South Africa, and nobody was treating the country's real citizens, the indigenous black people, in any decent way.

You could say Canada redeemed itself as far as South Africa goes when John Diefenbaker raised the necessary stink at the Commonwealth conference in London in 1961 over the apartheid regime in South Africa, which at the time was trying to weasel its way back into the organization. The U.S. barely paid attention to South Africa in 1961, and President Kennedy was still keeping a comfortable distance from civil rights efforts in the Deep South so he wouldn't lose political ground. To our credit, we kept fairly consistent pressure on the racist regime ahead of the U.S. and other Western powers.

Canada Goes Caribbean

The U.S. has Hawaii, Puerto Rico, Guam, the United States Virgin Islands, American Samoa and a few other South Pacific islands. We haven't gotten around to collecting any colonies yet. We've thought about it, though. Hey, sometimes a Caribbean island wants to claim us.

In 1917, Robert Borden went sailing through the Turks and Caicos Islands and decided we should have them. They were a British colony that got handed from Jamaica to the Bahamas before finally being left on their own, more or less, remaining part of the British West Indies with Mother England looking after their defence. Nothing came of Borden's efforts.

Then in 1974, a backbencher MP from Waterloo, Max Saltsman, noticed all the Canadians heading down there—about 16,000 each year, with more than 30 percent of the hotels owned by Canadians—and drafted a private member's bill to annex the islands so our tourist dollars would stay in Canada. It was a rather peculiar idea to come from an NDP member. Never submitted for a vote, the bill was controversial, with many folks liking the idea of a new Caribbean flavour to the Dominion, while others thought it smacked of colonialism. The idea faded away....

Until 1987, when Winnipeg MP Dan McKenzie revived the notion, only to have it squashed by fellow Tory David Daubney, who chaired a committee looking into the idea and called it "most inappropriate." Dan McKenzie, however, wasn't about to drop it; after he retired from politics, Brian Mulroney let him go on a fact-finding mission to the islands in 1989. (Some wags think it was to get him out of the country, where he'd be less annoying.) He returned, offering his report "on practical measures"— then died of a heart attack that same year.

Cut to 2004, when Peter Goldring, another Tory MP, rose in the House of Commons to say it was time Turks and Caicos became our 11th province. The problem with that was you have to go through the winding processes of the Canadian Constitution—and nobody wants that. The answer? Become part of an existing province, or so thought all three parties in Nova Scotia. They voted in favour of a non-binding resolution in the hopes it would jumpstart Ottawa.

Prime Minister Paul Martin spoke by phone with the Islands' Premier Michael Misick and invited him to Ottawa for talks, but still nothing came of it. "Every week we are on Canadian television and CNN and so on and tourists are coming here to see this island that Canadians say they want," said Misick. "If we were to quantify the business that we got since we started talking about Canada, you are talking about $15 million or $20 million, and you cannot pay for that."

And on the debate goes. In March 2009, Donna Jacobs mused in the *Ottawa Citizen*, "Suppose Canada built itself a deep-water port in the turquoise waters of the Caribbean...Suppose Canada did all this with its usual low-key, good-cop approach to world politics and regional strife, drawing on the goodwill that comes from its 100-year trading relationship in the Caribbean. (Canada's direct investment holdings in the Caribbean-Latin American market in 2007 totalled $87.2 billion)."

But the waters are always turquoise on the other side of the Gulf of Mexico. Only days after Jacobs pondered the benefits of Canada buying new beachfront property, the BBC reported that Britain would suspend self-government in the Turks and Caicos Islands, after the Foreign Office did some digging with a Commission of Inquiry and found "clear signs of political amorality and immaturity and of a general administrative incompetence." The same Michael Misick who chatted with Paul Martin, asking to join Canada, was accused of building up "a multi-million dollar fortune since coming to power in 2003" and selling Crown land to line his own pockets. The scandal prompted Misick to leave office, and Britain assumed direct control of its territory, promising elections in July 2011 or earlier.

So we might want to wait a little longer before we get our own colony-province-whatever-we're-thinking-of-calling-it in the tradition of Britain, France and the United States.

SEVEN
Religion

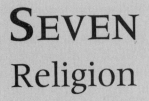

MORE GOD-LOVING
THAN GOD-FEARING

IN CANADA, THE MONUMENTS OF our religious tolerance are literal brick and mortar ones—the Orthodox onion domes of the Prairies, the Sikh temples of BC and that stunning hand-carved Hindu temple in Toronto. So it shouldn't surprise anyone that, in terms of numbers, we're at least as open-minded as Americans when it comes to religion. Some of us might expect that we would do better, but according to a study in 2009 by Gallup and a UK charity group called the Coexist Foundation, the Yanks outperform us at "integrating" their population into "interfaith cohesion." Its definition of "isolated" is "those who are unlikely to be members of any particular faith group and who tend to believe in the truth of their perspective above all others. They do not want to know about other religions. They also neither respect nor feel respected by those of other faiths."

Notice anything strange about that definition? Don't worry, we'll come back to it.

Of so-called tolerant populations, ones that live and let live but who don't likely learn from or about other religions, Canada has 50 percent while the U.S. has 52 percent. Then there's the category of "Integrated," which Gallup considers to be people who "believe that most faiths make a positive contribution to society. Furthermore, integrated people do not only feel respect toward people from other faith traditions, but they also feel respected by them." Canada had 31 percent of these integrated people while the U.S. had 33 percent.

Not to pick on a survey in which we're doing well, but it's good to remember that Gallup only sampled a thousand people. On its web page, it nicely gives itself an escape clause by stating, "In addition to sampling error, question wording and practical difficulties in conducting surveys can introduce error or bias into the findings of public opinion polls."

Well, no kidding. Much as one could pick at the stats in the rest of this book, it's interesting that Gallup's five questions included asking for agreement or disagreement with the following statements: " Most religious faiths make a positive contribution to society," and "In the past year, I have learned something from someone of another religious faith."

Recognize the potential problem yet? Go back to the definition of "isolated": those who are unlikely to be members of any particular faith group and who tend to believe in the truth of their perspective above all others. They do not want to know about other religions.

Is this Gallup's way of identifying agnostics and atheists, by any chance? And what is it with the little dig about "their perspective above all others"?

The implication of the survey questions is that if you don't want to know about religion in general, let alone specifics of one outside your culture, this is a bad thing. In the world of Gallup and the foundation, you are only "tolerant" if you belong to an organized religion. And it presumes those who belong to another faith always have wisdom to impart to us. *Maclean's* magazine promptly reported Gallup's findings in its "Canada versus the World" article in 2009 with barely a pause over its curious methodology.

Lest anyone out there think too much is being made of this, consider that there's a substantial portion of Canadians who either don't believe in God or prefer to visit with God when it fits their schedules. (God can make our three o' clock on Tuesday—She's everywhere, right?) More than 4 million of us self-identify as having "no religion," putting us in the number two spot behind Roman Catholics (at more than 12 million) and ahead of our leading Protestant denomination, the United Church. StatsCan reports "Between 1985 and 2004, the share of Canadians aged 15 and older reporting no religious affiliation increased by 7 percentage points from 12 percent to 19 percent. In addition, a growing share of Canadians had not attended any religious services in the previous year, even though they reported an affiliation...."

Does that make us less spiritual? Not necessarily. StatsCan claimed "many Canadians [mostly older ones] who infrequently or never attend services...regularly engage in personal religious practices." We like our spirituality and religion on our terms.

More head scratching over Gallup's tolerance figures may be needed when you consider that in 2007, Gallup reported on another poll in the U.S. on faith. It found that one third of the American adult population believes the Christian Bible should be taken literally word for word. Then it mentioned breezily how "a literal belief structure has been the basis for justifications for a variety of important positions in American life," which it listed as evolution taught in schools, same-sex marriage, the issue of whether only men should be preachers and priests, plus other topics.

That somehow doesn't jive with a 52 percent tolerance rate a mere two years later, does it? Especially when Gallup says Americans' views on the Bible haven't changed in 16 years. But as pointed out, Gallup has an interesting way to define tolerance.

CANADA'S CHRISTIAN RIGHT:
"FIVE DECADES OF DEFEAT"

IF WE'RE MORE QUESTIONING AND more personal in our faith, we Canadians also keep our church separate than our state, thank you very much, as opposed to our southern neighbours.

The U.S. has had to put up with the political power bases of fundamentalist icons like Billy Graham, who had the ear of several presidents and was later revealed to be an anti-Semite (Jews, Graham said to Richard Nixon in 1972, had a "stranglehold" on the media); Pat Robertson, who has called Hinduism "demonic"; Anita Bryant, a virulent homophobe who equated gays with pedophiles (she claimed they wanted to "recruit the youth of America"); and Jerry Falwell, who revealed over time he could spew hate pretty much in every direction. Falwell's targets over the course of decades included Jews, Muslims, Martin Luther King (he questioned King's "sincerity" and called him "left wing"), gays, Africans (he once called Bishop Desmond Tutu a "phoney" and told Christians they should reinvest in apartheid South Africa), Teletubbies, Bill Clinton, labour unions and victims of 9/11. Falwell publicly suggested that pagans, feminists and the American Civil Liberties Union, among others, were trying to "secularise" America and helped prompt the attacks on the Twin Towers and the Pentagon.

When Falwell died in 2007, Christopher Hitchens in *Slate* turned his literary laser on the preacher's corpse, highlighting for us the sharp difference between how we politically view our religious leaders compared to the Americans. Hitchens, being British, could make it plain for his U.S. audience that the emperor had no halo: "In his dingy racist past, Falwell attacked those churchmen who mixed the two worlds of faith and politics and called for civil rights. Then he realized that two could play at this game and learned to play it himself. Then he won the Republican Party over to the idea of religious voters and faith-based fund raising. And now, by example at least, he has inspired emulation in many Democrats and liberals who would like to borrow the formula. His place on the cable shows will be amply filled by Al Sharpton, another person who can get away with anything under the rubric of Reverend."

Interestingly, some have tried such tactics in Canada, but they just won't take. In reviewing the book, *Standing on Guard for Thee: The Past, Present and Future of Canada's Christian Right* in 2008, Michael Valpy in the *Literary Review of Canada* noted how the author "catalogues five decades of defeat on the battlefields of feminism, the sexual revolution, abortion and homosexuality. He records how, time and again, the hopes of the Canadian Christian right are raised only to be dashed. Conservative Brian Mulroney turns out to be as socially liberal as Pierre Trudeau...Christian social conservatives are shocked to learn that two-thirds of delegates to the Reform Party's 1992 national assembly respond to a questionnaire by saying they believe abortion is a private matter of choice between a woman and her doctor...Ralph Klein lets them down by refusing to use the Charter's notwithstanding clause to get around the Supreme Court's decision requiring an amendment to Alberta's human rights legislation forbidding discrimination on the grounds of sexual orientation. Stephen Harper punishes members of his caucus who speak out against homosexuality."

When it comes to faith, whether one agrees with liberal politics or not is deemed to be beside the issue.

As the subhead for Valpy's piece in the *Literary Review* put it, "In this country, it seems, we really *do* like our religion kept private." And it's somewhat interesting— perhaps encouraging to many—that we haven't had a Billy Graham/Jerry Falwell power broker emerge on our political landscape (thank Krishna). The thunder got robbed early, considering that our largest Protestant denomination, the United Church, allowed for the ordination of women in 1936 (and the Anglican Church allowed for it in 1974), while also backing gay rights, same-sex marriage and access to abortion in rural areas. So you might well wonder how you build a political power base of God-fearing Christians in a country in which God is...well, love.

After all, it was Tommy Douglas, a Baptist minister who preached in Weyburn, Saskatchewan, who became the father of that most hated of liberal policy planks: universal health care in Canada.

EIGHT
Sports

CHECK THE
SCOREBOARD

IT'S ALL OVER NOW, BUT WHILE this book was being written, we were saturated with tiresome commercials pushing the 2010 Winter Olympics in Vancouver, all asking again and again, "Do you believe?" Which I always felt carried a note of increasing desperation. Do you believe? Do you? Come on, do you believe? Clap your hands together, boys and girls! Clap your hands! Tinkerbell will come back to life after the luge ran over her!

Hey, CTV, we don't have to believe. We already *know* we're good at sports. And not just the kind on ice and snow.

After all, one of our guys from Almonte, Ontario, Dr. James Naismith invented basketball all the way back in 1891. He needed a new indoor sport for the students at the YMCA college in Springfield, Massachusetts, so that they could remain active in winter. Trust a Canadian to know how to get around winter.

More than a whole century later, basketball has become a quintessentially American sport, with a Toronto team in the form of the Raptors only squeezing their way into the NBA in 1995 (while the absolutely awful Vancouver Grizzlies were finally put out of their misery in 2000 when the franchise was sold to Memphis). But as a people, we have been catching up.

For instance, Steve Nash—who was born in South Africa but grew up in Victoria—besieged American universities with letters so he could play Division 1 ball. U.S. schools didn't have much faith in the hoop dreams of a Canuck kid, not until California's Santa Clara University offered him a scholarship. His pro point guard career had a rocky start (in his rookie year, he only averaged about 10 minutes a game), but it really took off when he changed back from the Dallas Mavericks to the original team that drafted him, the Phoenix Suns. Nash won the NBA's Most Valuable Player award two years in a row in 2005 and 2006, which puts him in the ranks of legendary Magic Johnson and Michael Jordan.

We have our moments, too, with other sports you normally think of as simply American ones. In 2003, Mike Weir of Sarnia, Ontario, became the first Canadian male golfer to win the Masters Tournament. In 1968, Sandra Post of Oakville, Ontario, was the first Canadian to play the LPGA Championship—and she won it.

If you want to be generous and extend "Canadian athletes" past humans, what about our thoroughbred, Northern Dancer? He's the most successful sire in North American history, with 146 stakes winners around the world! He won at the Kentucky Derby, then the Preakness, in 1964. Yes, a horse is a horse, of course— but this one was the first of his species ever inducted into the Canadian Sports Hall of Fame.

You don't want to talk nags? Fine, let's talk cars.

We can run laps around the Americans with the racing dynasty of the Villeneuves. Québec's Gilles Villeneuve is still remembered as one of Formula One's most tenacious drivers, whom Niki Lauda called "the craziest devil" he ever came across. In an all-too-brief career, he racked up six wins and two poles in six seasons and finished second by four points in the 1979 world championship to teammate Jody Scheckter. His son, Jacques, won the Indianapolis 500 in 1995 and the Formula One World Championship in 1997. That puts him in select company—he's the only other driver after Mario Andretti and Emerson Fittipaldi to win both.

We've got sports achievements we barely remember—but should because they balance us quite nicely against all those American trophies. And of course, we've got the showstoppers everyone remembers. Here are just a few.

Phil Edwards: Man of Bronze

Everyone's heard of Jesse Owens, the black American who showed up the "Master Race" in Berlin's 1936 Olympics, with a fuming Hitler walking out as Owens received his medal. But a black Canadian, Phil Edwards, was there as well to prove Hitler wrong.

Edwards was originally from British Guyana, and although he set a number of intercollegiate records when he ran for New York University, he didn't qualify for the U.S. Olympic team. In 1927, Melville Robinson, the manager of Canada's Olympic track and field team invited him to run for us. (Robinson himself is an important Canadian sports figure, having organized the first ever Commonwealth Games, which were held in Hamilton, Ontario, in 1930; back then they were known as, ahem, the "British Empire Games.") Edwards picked up his first bronze medal, as part of Canada's relay team, at the 1928 Summer Olympics in Amsterdam.

After that, he went to McGill University to study medicine—not the easiest subject when you're trying to remain a competitive athlete. And yet in his six years at McGill, he found the time to compete in every intercollegiate championship. As captain of the Canadian track and field team at the Los Angeles Olympics in 1932, he picked up bronzes for three races and collected another for the 800-metre event at the Berlin Games in 1936. With five medals, our "man of bronze" racked up a collection that wasn't matched until Marc Gagnon's speed-skating performance in 2002.

When Edwards was on his way home from Berlin, he had a stop in London, but the hotel where his team was booked refused to give him a room. To their credit, the rest of the team quickly repacked their bags and cancelled their stay *en masse*, heading with Edwards to book elsewhere. "If this hotel is too good for Phil Edwards," declared fencer Cathleen Hughes-Hallett, "it's too good for me."

As a doctor, Phil Edwards went on to become a highly respected expert in tropical diseases and took part in several international medical missions.

"Touch 'em All, Joe!"

Say it loud and proud: two—count 'em, two—World Series wins by the Toronto Blue Jays. Their first Series triumph, against the Atlanta Braves in 1992, was dramatic enough, with Atlanta coming within one run in the bottom of the 11th, and Jays reliever Mike Timlin fielding a bunt by Otis Nixon, hurling it to Joe Carter at first base for the final out. It was the first time America's favourite pastime championship went to a team outside the United States.

Then a year later, as the Jays battled the Phillies, another heartstopper. With a count of two balls and two strikes, the Phillies' Mitch Williams pitched a low fastball that Joe Carter rocketed down the left-field line and over the wall for a three-run homer. As Carter made his tour around the bases, 54,000 fans stood and cheered, with Jays players mobbing Carter as he reached home plate. Not only were the Jays the first team in 16 years to clinch the Series twice, this was the second time ever in baseball history for the Series to end with a home run.

On radio, veteran broadcaster Tom Cheek yelled, "Touch 'em all, Joe! You'll never hit a bigger home run in your life!" He was right.

We could already pat ourselves on the back for the Montréal Expos winning the National League Division title in 1981. Then the Jays showed their first triumph in 1985 when they beat the Yankees to go into the American League championship against Kansas City. Since then, we've had Ferguson Jenkins join the Hall of Fame in 1991 and Jason Bay win Rookie of the Year in 2004. But Canada was making baseball history before we even had a major league team here.

Fans know Jackie Robinson started in the major leagues with the Brooklyn Dodgers, but his debut with the Montréal Royals in April 1946 was when he really started changing history. It was the first time a black man played in a triple-A minor league game, and Robinson hit a three-run homer that day and finished with four hits and two stolen bases (oh, by the way, Montréal creamed the New York Giants 14–1). At a Royals home game with 16,000 fans packed into Delorimier Stadium, Robinson got the biggest ovation of any Montréal player. True, Jackie Robinson became an American baseball legend, but Canadians first made him feel at home on the diamond.

Because James Bisson put it better in *One Hundred Greatest Canadian Sports Moments,* we'll let him say it: "Many, including Robinson, doubt it would ever have happened had it not been for the city of Montréal, which welcomed the star second baseman into the community with open arms and an attitude of tolerance that simply didn't exist in his native country."

You Win a Cold War on the Ice

The names say it all: Gordie Howe, Wayne Gretzky, Mario Lemieux, Daryl Sittler, so many others...and of course, Bobby Orr, who really got the Americans to pay attention. In 1970, with 120 points racked up during his 1969–70

Top 10 Canadian Hockey Players of All Time

Name	Playing Career	Career NHL Totals				Place of Birth
		Games Played	Goals	Assists	Points	
Wayne Gretzky	1979-1999	1487	894	1963	2857	Brantford, Ontario
Gordie Howe	1946-1997	1767	801	1049	1850	Flora, Saskatchewan
Marcel Dionne	1971-1989	1348	731	1040	1771	Drummondville, Québec
Mario Lemieux	1984-2006	915	690	1033	1723	Montreal, Québec
Phil Esposito	1963-1981	1282	717	873	1590	Sault Ste. Marie, Ontario
Ray Bourque	1979-2001	1612	410	1169	1579	Saint-Laurent, Québec
Paul Coffey	1980-2000	1409	396	1135	1531	Weston, Ontario
Bryan Trottier	1975-1994	1279	524	901	1425	Val Marie, Saskatchewan
Johhny Bucyk	1955-1978	1540	556	813	1369	Edmonton, Alberta
Guy Lafleur	1971-1991	1127	560	793	1353	Thurso, Québec

season, Orr became the first hockey player to be named *Sports Illustrated*'s Sportsman of the Year.

We have the greatest hockey players who ever lived, but on a team level it's hard to be smug when there are only six Canadian-based franchises in a 30-team league. Still, in 1989, we had an all-Canadian Stanley Cup final when the Calgary Flames beat the Montréal Canadiens. We also won the Canada Cup four out of five times, beating out five other nations, between 1976 and 1991.

And let's face it, as many times as an American hockey league franchise may win the Stanley Cup, they'll never have anything to equal the 1972 Summit Series, when Team Canada beat the Soviet Union.

With that one, we won a Cold War all by ourselves.

A Canadian at Heart

"When I was growing up and going to boxing tournaments, Canada was never considered a strong boxing nation," says Lennox Lewis. "And I always wondered, 'Why were all these guys ranked ahead of me? Just because they came from another country?'"

Born in the West Ham district of London, England, from the age of 12 Lewis grew up in Kitchener. Although he later would go pro in Britain, he was proud to represent Canada as a super heavyweight amateur in the 1984 Olympics in Los Angeles. Years later, *Sports Illustrated* snidely reported that "many Brits continue to regard him as a Canadian at heart and a Briton for convenience." In LA, Lewis advanced all the way to the quarter-finals, only to lose to American Tyrell Biggs. Lewis could have turned pro then. Many folks asked, why wait four more years before another chance for a medal? But Lewis chose to wait.

In Seoul in 1988, he got his gold. He pummelled American Riddick Bowe with a right-hook to the side of the head, prompting a second standing count in the match and the referee to finally stop the fight. But there's an interesting sequel to this Canadian-American battle. It turned into a small feud. After collecting heavyweight titles for Europe, Britain and the Commonwealth, Lewis was all set as the number one contender to take on then-champion Bowe for the World Boxing Championship Belt in 1992. But Bowe ducked Lewis in the pros and held a news conference during which he petulantly tossed his WBC belt in a trashcan to avoid a mandatory defence of his title. The WBC didn't think much of his stunt and declared Lewis its champion in January 1993.

Lewis had the good sense and class to retire in 2004 while still on top. When the rumour mill started grinding again over a rematch with Bowe, he was quietly dismissive. "He waits until I am in retirement to call out my name. I will come out of retirement to beat up that guy. I'll beat him up for free."

Lewis was inducted into Canada's Sports Hall of Fame in 2008.

Donovan Bailey: World's Fastest Man

There. We gave him the title, which he earned and rightly had coming after he won the 100-metre race at the Atlanta Olympics in 1996. Traditionally, the casual title "World's Fastest Man" goes to he who collects the gold from the 100 metres. And Bailey, who collected a second gold in Atlanta for Canada's relay team, did a lot to banish the cloud of disgrace over the Ben Johnson scandal. "Everywhere I go, people still remind me about that race," says Bailey. "Canadians are always telling me how much they appreciated my performance. I feel very blessed to have accomplished what I did."

But in 1997, American Michael Johnson—who won gold for both the 200 metre and 400 metre races in Atlanta—started calling himself the "World's Fastest Man" in commercials. Gradually, as these things do, ordinary sports fans and media types began to question Johnson calling himself this, until the controversy took on a momentum of its own. It didn't matter that Bailey broke Olympic and World records with his new 100-metre time of 9.84 seconds. Johnson supporters go on and on about how if you divide the American's 200 metre time of 19.32 seconds in two, you get 9.66, which is less than Bailey's time of 9.84 and blah, blah, blah...(check out Wikipedia if you want to see the rationalizing).

We don't want to hear it. It's not the same event. Simple as that.

Bailey's initial response over the issue was to reply, "The world's fastest man was decided in Atlanta."

The bio on his own website sums up candidly what happened next: "But after some highly publicized trash-talk between the two, a made-for-TV 150-metre showcase was announced. The identity of the World's Fastest Man would be decided in Toronto."

Sixty thousand fans sold out the SkyDome to see what amounted to grudge match meets media circus. On the curving track, Johnson pulled up lame at the 110-metre mark, later claiming he injured his quadriceps, and as Bailey dashed ahead, about to finish, he looked over his shoulder at Johnson, waving him to "Come on!"— perhaps thinking his rival had given up. You can still see an old CBS sports clip of the race floating around YouTube, complete with American commentators still rationalizing beforehand how Johnson was technically faster. Way to be impartial in your coverage.

But it didn't matter. Although, at 14.99 seconds, Bailey didn't make his best time, he won—and collected the $1.5 million prize. As the Sports section of the *Toronto Star* put it in 2008, "it left all those in the SkyDome glowing. More important, it shut America up."

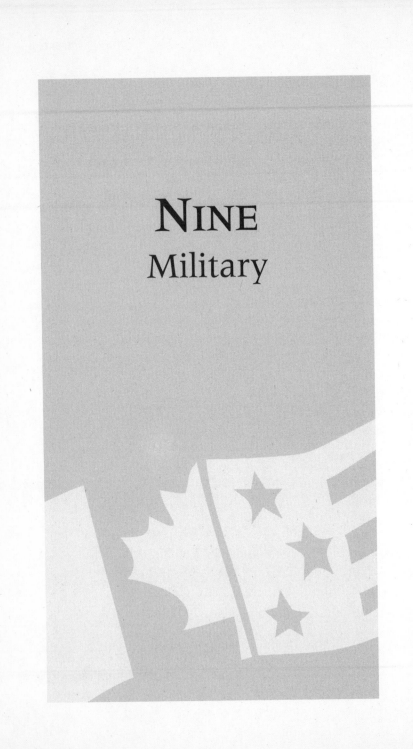

NINE
Military

WE DO MORE BEFORE
6:00 AM THAN MOST FOLKS CAN DO OVER 244,000 KM OF COASTLINE

THE OLD JOKE HAS BEEN THAT our tiny army could be out-classed by the New York police force if the Americans ever wanted to invade. I always thought this was a bad analogy, because two nights in the Québec wilderness at −15° C would send d'ose bums back to Brooklyn, you know what I'm talkin' 'bout? Of course, they could invade in the summer, in which case, maybe the black-flies will get 'em. And as someone will quickly point out, all they'd really want is our big cities, the Great Lakes and the freshwater. Ah, but we're a nation of campers! We'd hold out. Sure.

Well, maybe not. Patriotic types often suggest, as one columnist did in 2009, that our country is perfect for guerrilla warfare. True, but only if you were fighting before 1950. On that score, let's just say thermal imaging is a beautiful thing.

But I think I've come across the ultimate argument for why the U.S. should never try to invade us and why scores of right-wing types, from the *National Review*'s Jonah Goldberg to Ann Coulter, ought to knock it off about "allowing" us to be in North America, casually bombing us and moving in (see page 256). They always assume it's an "us versus them" fight.

Guess what, right-wing neighbours. A very large portion of the rest of the world doesn't like you. They do like Canada. How about we work out a few nice trade agreements with other parties and invite them to come over as a multinational defence force to help our small army? Maybe we'll talk to China and invoke the name of Norman Bethune a couple of times. Maybe we'll ask the Dutch to help—they're still grateful to us. Or maybe we'll suggest to Britain we convert you back so that most of North America can be part of the Commonwealth.

All kidding aside, if you put the question of possible invasion from America to anyone in the Canadian Armed Forces, they'll promptly reply the U.S. is a valued ally, and we don't want to fight them anyway, especially when they have more than 1,500,000 active fighting personnel, and the U.S. Department of Defense didn't even blink when it asked in 2009 for more than $515 *billion* for its base budget. We don't have the people, and we don't have the money.

But we do have the heart. Remember, our navy guys and gals have to protect one of the longest coastlines anywhere, in the second biggest country in the world. There's a lot to defend, but thankfully, we don't have that many folks out there who want to hurt us. We've had only one recent war to cope with, while the Americans have been fighting two, Afghanistan and Iraq, and one of those was a sequel. We also eliminated a long time ago a silly orientation problem so that we don't ask, we don't tell, we don't care—our personnel just get on with the job (see page 20).

NO, WE ARE NOT
PEACEKEEPERS ANYMORE

SERIOUSLY, GET THAT WARM AND gushy image of us out of your head, because it just ain't true. Since 1948, we've actually committed fewer than 100 military and civilian police for dozens of peacekeeping missions, and often it was fewer than 10 personnel. But we still spend a lot on our defence. Canada's military budget for 2008 was $18.2 billion—which is tiny, of course, when compared to the U.S., which spent $607 billion in 2008 and topped the world's military spenders that year according to the Stockholm International Peace Research Institute. But if we come up a peashooter next to the American cannon, we're no slouch when it comes to NATO—as one of the organization's 26 member countries, Canada is sixth in total military spending.

Canadian doves might be surprised—and worried—to know that according to the Institute, we're also one of the largest arms suppliers in the world and were ranked 15th largest in 2009. Canadian bullets, guidance systems, aircraft parts and trucks are worth an estimated $7 billion a year and go everywhere from China to Saudi Arabia. If the eagle prefers to hold its wings protectively over parts of the world, the beaver likes to build and sell dams overseas.

FIGHTING CANUCKS

THE NUMBERS BREAK DOWN LIKE THIS: in the Canadian Forces Regular Force, there are almost 67,000 personnel, with more than 35,000 in the Primary Reserve; we have more than 20,000 individuals in the air force, more than 35,000 persons in the army and about 11,000 personnel in the navy. On paper, at least, you can see we're in a complete state of battle readiness...to invade Luxembourg. Okay, we're not that bad. And there's a plan underway for the Canadian Forces to expand to around 100,000 by 2027.

As far as equipment goes, our navy currently has 33 warships, submarines and coastal defence vessels split up between the Atlantic and Pacific Coasts. Our army has everything from an armoured mobile bridge "launcher" called—no kidding—"The Beaver" to howitzers and Leopard tanks. And our air force has jets like the CC-150 Polaris, which has been used for long-range transport in Afghanistan. For its part, just trust—because armies don't like to tell you exactly how many toys they have—that the U.S. has thousands of tanks; after all, they have to outfit more than a million active personnel.

Both Americans and Canadians, of course, serve overseas, although G.I. Joe casts a much bigger shadow across the world: the U.S. Armed Forces has more than 266,000 of its people in 80 countries. If you look carefully at their deployment, however, you might scratch your head at some of the choices. Back in spring 2008, the U.S. still had more than 56,000 personnel just for Germany, which makes you wonder if the Bush administration got the memo that the Cold War was over. You also have to wonder why the U.S. needed nine military personnel in Burma, a country it has imposed sanctions on and where, at best, its presence is highlighted by an embassy on Merchant Street in Yangon (Rangoon).

Kenya had 40 Americans, while troubled Sudan had only three. *Three*. That's it. In a nation where the Khartoum regime has systematically tried to exterminate its southern black population and its leader was declared a war criminal by an international court, Canada has committed up to 50 military personnel and 25 civilian police officers to peacekeeping operations there (with security efforts, plus aid, plus reconstruction, we've ponied up more than $674 million since 2006 for that country alone).

Although there are fewer of us, we spread out and make our efforts count elsewhere, too. According to the DND website, "On any given day, about 8000 Canadian Forces members—one third of our deployable force—are preparing for, engaged in or returning from an overseas mission." Canadian military personnel have served in some of the hottest trouble spots of the world, including Congo, Sierra Leone, Cyprus, Haiti, the Balkans and the Golan Heights. So maybe size doesn't matter—maybe we should look at the record.

WE STAND ON GUARD
FOR THEE, BUT WE ALSO KICK ASS

AFTER CANADIAN LIEUTENANT ANDREW Leslie suggested Canada's military might need a year to recover when its deployment in Afghanistan winds down in 2011, a broadcast nobody on Fox News exiled to the network's graveyard slot decided to weigh in and casually insult us. "Isn't this the perfect time to invade this ridiculous country?" host Greg Gutfeld asked his panel of guests in 2009. "They have no army!"

"I didn't even know they were in the war," mocked guest Doug Benson as four more troops slain in the conflict were taken home to Canada. Then he suggested we're the nation you run to when you want to avoid fighting. Benson had forgotten that he was due to fly up and perform his stand-up act soon in the very place he was insulting—gigs that were quickly cancelled when Canadians saw his remarks repeated on YouTube, CBC and CTV.

Gutfeld's guests, all thinking they were very clever in the moment of the broadcast, decided Canada hides under the blanket of security of its southern neighbour. Gutfeld asked, "Would Canada be able to get away with this if they didn't share a border with the most powerful country in the universe?"

Not only did Fox reap a storm of angry emails and phone calls, but Ottawa weighed in and demanded an apology, pointing out the obvious about our soldiers lost and our fighting in some of the toughest sectors. Fox—which hardly ever apologizes to anyone, even when it implied again and again that the elected U.S. president wasn't born in his own country—actually back-pedalled fast over the embarrassing ignorance of its host. The Moose had roared.

Gutfeld wound up giving two apologies. One was a statement that claimed the remarks "may have been misunderstood" and weren't meant to disrespect our "brave" soldiers. Then on camera, like a smirking brat of a six-year-old who can't understand why he's being yelled at for peeing on the carpet, Gutfeld said, "However, as a light-hearted show with a satirical view, we sometimes go over the line, and in this case, I *obviously* (his emphasis) did not intend to offend your national pride and love of military service. I apologize."

Well, no, Gutfeld, you obviously did intend to offend. And we all know you did.

Certainly not every American is so shamelessly ignorant, and many do appreciate us, but for those times when you run into a small collection who don't, here's a primer of where we've done our part—and quite often done more than the U.S. military.

The "Madmen" of the Great War

This was one of the stupidest wars of modern times, in which men died in bloody battles of slaughter—like the Somme—for nothing. Nobody can claim there was any heroic purpose or that we were fighting for any noble cause. But American textbooks would have you believe their troops showed up and resolved the whole mess through sheer force of thousands of fresh troops, which just ain't true. What really broke the stalemate was the tank, an innovation pushed for by a Brit—*the* iconic Brit—Winston Churchill, when he was First Lord of the Admiralty. (Yeah, yeah, I know we're talking tanks, and yet he was heading the Admiralty, which is sea stuff. Just go hit the library if you need to know more.)

The Americans entered the war on April 6th, 1917, which means they fought for less than two years. We were in it from the beginning.

We became the shock troops for the British in numerous battles, with the Germans thinking these prairie boys and lumberjacks-turned-soldiers were downright insane, they were so fierce. "The British, they are good soldiers but the Canadians, they are madmen," declared one German officer taken prisoner. We were the masters of the night raid, and sometimes all it took was a single Canadian private to escort in at the end of his rifle a dozen or more disarmed prisoners. If you don't believe it, go read the excellent two-volume history of Canada in the war, *At the Sharp End* and *Shock Troops*, by Tim Cook.

We fought longer and suffered a more substantial loss. More than 60,000 Canadians lost their lives when our population during the Great War was a little more than seven million. By 1918, the year the war ended, the U.S. already had a population of more than 103 million—and all their wartime casualties were a little more than 53,000.

World War Two: In the Thick of It

The next time you catch *Saving Private Ryan* as the late late-night movie, remember that when the 3rd Canadian Division and 2nd Canadian Armoured Brigade landed on Juno Beach on June 6, 1944, in the Battle of Normandy, we were in the thick of it. By the end of D-Day, Canadian troops had penetrated deeper into France than either the British or the Americans at their landing points. The only soldiers getting worse resistance were at Omaha Beach.

Canada's involvement was crucial and reached several different facets of the conflict. Twenty Canadian pilots gave their lives to help win the Battle of Britain. Seventy-two of our merchant marine ships were lost to enemy action. While Canada wasn't big in the Pacific Theatre, two Canadian battalions fought to defend Hong Kong, and fewer than 1500 soldiers survived the ordeal of combat and the nightmares of Japanese prison camps and slave labour. You better believe our guys made sacrifices.

In July 1943, Canadians invaded Sicily and hit mainland Italy to drive the Germans out in a bitter struggle, at times in street-by-street fighting. As historian Desmond Morton puts it in *A Military History of Canada*, "At Boulogne, Calais and Le Havre, Canadians staged bloody, destructive sieges...." When Field Marshall Montgomery decided to let his advance guard sit around Antwerp, it was up to the Canadians to help clear the blocked ports in the Battle of the Scheldt, which cost us 3500 lives. When the Allies fought their way into Germany, we were there with our 4th Canadian Armoured Division.

Canadians were the ones who liberated Holland in the spring of 1945 (we also kept their Princess Juliana safe in our country during the war), and Holland has kept affectionate ties with Canada ever since. The tulips you see on Parliament Hill come from a crop of 100,000 hand-picked bulbs from a grateful people. In his bestseller, *Who Killed Canadian History?*, J.L. Granatstein movingly writes of the enduring gratitude of the Dutch. For the 50th commemoration of V-E Day in Apeldoorn in 1995, broadcast live by the CBC, Granatstein recalls, "There were astonishing, wrenchingly emotional events that left me and many of those who participated in them in tears much of the time." And the people of Holland are still grateful and still remember the Canadian war effort to this day—they keep a better memory of it in many ways than Canadians themselves.

This little summary barely scratches the surface of Canada's contribution during the war. The bottom line, however, is that we were in it earlier than the Americans, fought just as hard and gave our all, with more than 42,000 soldiers making the supreme sacrifice.

The Korean War and Holding the Line at Kapyong

For background, all you need to know is there might never have been a war in the first place if Britain, the Soviet Union and the U.S. hadn't decided to carve up Korea at the Potsdam Conference in 1945 without consulting the folks who actually lived there. When the war started in the summer of 1950, the Americans called it a "police action"—which became a snide joke in countless *M*A*S*H* episodes—because Congress never formally declared it on behalf of the U.S. It was all under a UN umbrella for the supposedly democratic South Korean side ruled by political strongman Syngman Rhee, (see page 115), with the U.S. in charge of the military operations.

When America wanted our help, Canadians enthusiastically stepped up to go fight. Hundreds of men hit the recruiting centres before they were even set to open. In fact, our troops arrived just a few days after Communist China invaded in November 1950 to help the North.

But the conflict became a mess that was like an Asian version of the Great War. A stalemate. One soldier described finishing his tour of defending a hill, only to sign up for a second tour two years later and be posted to the same familiar hill! Not one inch of progress. Military historian Desmond Morton put it best when he wrote, "On the whole, Canadians preferred to forget about Korea. The interminable ceasefire negotiations, punctuated by outbursts of fighting, served some inscrutable Communist purpose no one else could discern...If taxes rose and consumer spending was curbed, very few Canadians gave any evidence of suffering."

Canadians still brought their characteristic heroism to battle, even when the battle couldn't be won. In April 1951, when the Chinese sent about 700,000 men to try to retake Seoul, someone had to stand in their way. But the South Korean forces broke, and they and American units were in retreat. To help them get away and block the Chinese soldiers flooding in, the 3rd Battalion of the Royal Australian Regiment, plus a New Zealand regiment and our own 2nd Battalion of Princess Patricia's Canadian Light Infantry, had to hold their defensive positions at a place called Kapyong.

After hitting the Aussies hard, the Chinese turned on the Canadians, who held back wave after wave of the enemy throughout the night. By dawn the next day, an Australian major, Ben O'Dowd, had his radio operator try to contact help. But the American Marine Division refused to believe it was their allies, thinking it was the enemy in disguise! O'Dowd grabbed the phone and asked to speak to the man's commander, who also didn't believe that the Australians and Canadians could still be there—they had to have been wiped out.

"I've got news for you," snapped O'Dowd. "We are still here, and we are staying here."

The Australians held on until late into the day, when they finally had to withdraw with the New Zealand artillery giving them support. But the Canadians didn't budge. The Chinese stopped bothering to attack their positions altogether. By the afternoon of the following day, the road through to their forces was cleared completely of enemy soldiers. The Australian and Canadian battalions both received U.S. Presidential Distinguished Unit Citations for their part in the Battle of Kapyong.

Technically, the Korean War still isn't over. An armistice was agreed to, but no treaty has ever been signed.

In all, 25,000 Canadian soldiers served in Korea. They did their part to help the Americans and the UN in a doomed crusade to keep South Korea "democratic."

Vietnam: Pro, Anti—We Did Both

The Vietnam War is interesting because you can say we did our part to help no matter which side of the issue you're on. Don't worry, we'll explain.

Vietnam was a quagmire for Western powers the minute World War Two was over. You might vaguely remember the French had it as a colony, but if you really want to impress the American at the bar during your friendly argument, point out that the surrendering Japanese recognized a new government led by Ho Chi Minh, and then for a short time, the British briefly tried to hold things together there. Better still, point out that an American Office of Strategic Services team (the OSS, the forerunner to the CIA) actually met Ho and helped train his Viet Minh guerrillas in 1945! When the Americans brought along a Frenchman to test whether the Vietnamese would allow their former colonial masters back, Ho—who had lived in Brooklyn for a year— snapped in fluent English: "Look, who are you guys trying to kid? This man is not part of the deal." He had the Frenchman escorted back to the border.

The lieutenant in charge of OSS agents in Vietnam warned in a report that same year that "the French and British are finished here, and we ought to clear out of Southeast Asia."

So jump ahead about 20 years, and Canada wasn't that interested in fighting the spectre of Communism in what sounded like a replay of Korea. We never formally sent troops. Lester Pearson and his government showed remarkable synch with the growing public discomfort with the war, both here at home and south of the border. When in 1965 he was invited to speak at Temple University in Philadelphia, he suggested with his usual careful choice of words as a trained diplomat that the Americans ought to stop bombing North Vietnam into the Stone Age so that peace negotiations could finally get rolling.

Lyndon Johnson lost his temper so badly over the speech that the next day at Camp David he grabbed Pearson by the lapels and harangued him. The story goes that Pearson was shocked and rattled by the president's near violence, but our prime minister should get points for having the courage to speak his position and for holding his ground. When the Opposition taunted him in Parliament over what LBJ thought of his bombing pause suggestion, Pearson shot back flatly, "He was very interested in it, Mr. Speaker."

His wouldn't be the last Canadian government to lecture America over Vietnam. In 1973, Nixon escalated the bombing, hoping to pound the North into crawling back to the negotiation table. By then, Trudeau's minority government was in power, and a motion passed the House, condemning the prolonged hostilities. Nixon put Canada on his famous "shit list," and Canadian diplomats couldn't get in to meet with their American counterparts.

But as we mentioned before, we did our part no matter which side of the fence you're on.

Suppose you think going to war against North Vietnam was a good thing. Given hindsight and how Communists treated their people in various parts of the world, and how Cambodia turned into killing fields under a deranged maniac in charge of the Khmer Rouge, you have a case (of course, maybe if the U.S. hadn't helped destabilize the country by bombing the crap out of it, the Khmer

157

Rouge wouldn't have got so far—oops, okay, let's just stick with the idea you perhaps don't like Communism). Many Canadians believed the Communists had to be stopped in Southeast Asia. Some merely wanted adventure. The numbers are hard to pin down, with estimates ranging wildly from 10,000 to 40,000 Canucks signing up to serve in the American military during the war. We *were* there, albeit not officially, but many fought. In 1995, a monument of Canadian service in Vietnam, built by four Michigan men who used money out of their own pockets, was unveiled in Windsor.

Our Lady of Perpetual Sorrows from Bigoted Ignorance, Ann Coulter used these Canadians going off to fight as a way to prevaricate and talk her way out of being found wrong by Bob McKeown on *The Fifth Estate*. This came after she insisted Canada officially sent troops there and he corrected her (see page 176). The silly argument still goes on in Internet land, where the ignorant now claim Canada sent a "few hundred troops" under the UN's Operation Gallant. *Bzzzz*. Still wrong.

Canada sent 240 military personnel and 50 staff from External Affairs in 1973 to investigate compliance with the Paris Peace Treaty Agreement. And these personnel were there only from January 29 until July 31. Only in Coulter-land do foreign sign-ups and a limited investigative mission equate to being an active participant in an armed conflict. Since Iranian personnel took a turn and relieved our staff for the UN's operation, maybe the critics would like to host some veterans' events for the Iranians as well.

By 1970, Canada had taken in roughly 60,000 American draft dodgers and deserters. The dodgers tended to be middle-class, university-educated young people, while the deserters were more often than not from modest income backgrounds with barely half ever getting any education past high school, and that was often community college. As it turned out, we were a nice place to hole up, but these new arrivals didn't see themselves as immigrants.

As one commentator put it at the time, many Canadians grew to resent them as "hopelessly professional Americans who are detached from the mother country in name only, and do nothing to assimilate themselves into Canada." One professor at Carleton University demanded, "When are they going to begin asking what they can do for Canada, for *Canada's* primary problems, because the Vietnam War is not the only nor even the primary Canadian problem?" The *Toronto Star* profiled an organization for American dodgers and deserters in 1970 and noted that "to try and fit into Canadian life" ranked number five on its priority list.

For others, the answer was to never bother assimilating. Under Jimmy Carter, an amnesty in 1977 allowed many to go home. It's never been pinned down exactly how many took advantage of this window; most estimates are conservative and put it at 15 percent. If you want to look at it another way, maybe the new Americans saw the light and eventually Canadianized themselves in outlook and love of our country.

If you want to be negative and think all we are is a country where you go to avoid war, as Doug Benson suggested on Fox's show...well, have you ever heard of somebody having to desert *Canada* for the U.S. to avoid war?

Didn't think so.

Iraq: Are You Kidding?

Oh, please. We didn't buy it even before the suddenly vanishing weapons of mass destruction. It never made sense to go attack Saddam Hussein, who had nothing to do with 9/11, and who the Americans originally backed and even used as a hit-man (see page 116).

159

Columnist Ian Welsh rather niftily summed up our attitude to the Second Gulf War in *The Huffington Post*: "We don't believe that when Fred hits you, you should attack Mary instead just because you don't like Mary and always wanted to beat her bloody."

Afghanistan

Canadians are divided over whether we should be militarily involved in Afghanistan, and it doesn't help that, in 2009, there were allegations of vote-rigging in the re-election of Afghan President Hamid Karzai, and a senior Canadian diplomat suggested our top people in charge of the mission may have turned a blind eye to torture, which could damage our rep almost the same way Iraq's Abu Ghraib tainted the U.S. And we won't debate the issue here. No one doubts we are fighting a genuinely evil enemy. Psychopathic zealots who, among other things, blow up Buddhist works of art? Art that regular Muslim Afghans can recognize as part of a national heritage?

Captain Nancy Pelletier gives a Canadian flag kite to a child in Kabul

Yep, evil. Throwing acid into the faces of young Muslim girls merely trying to walk to school to get an education? Definitely evil. Of course, the Taliban have been perpetrating evil and committing human rights abuses in Afghanistan since 1996, but no one was in a hurry to save ordinary Afghans there prior to mid-September 2001.

Whether you believe we should be over there or that we should have stayed home, you can't say our troops haven't done a remarkable, amazing job, for which we all should be proud.

Before President Obama shifted the focus of the U.S. military to Afghanistan from Iraq, Peter Pigott wrote in 2007 for his authoritative *Canada in Afghanistan*: "To much of the world, the Afghan mission is discretionary, a sideshow. Nowhere is this attitude more evident than in the body count, with three countries—the United States, Canada and Britain—accounting for 90 percent of NATO's combat casualties. Americans killed in action account for half of the total, followed by Canada with 25 percent and Britain with 15 percent."

Now consider the blow of our sons and daughters lost in 2006 when looking at the tally of our troop contribution. The U.S. had sent in 11,800, the UK 6000 and Canada 2500. You better believe we feel it as a country when our soldiers are killed. As we go to press, more than 146 Canadian soldiers have lost their lives for the mission, as well as one Canadian diplomat and two Canadian aid workers. And as of late November 2009, Canada had 2830 Canadian Forces personnel deployed in Afghanistan.

Canada was helping Afghanistan even before the war—earmarking about $10 million in humanitarian aid each year. In the wake of 9/11, a battle unit from Princess Patricia's Canadian Light Infantry spent six months in Kandahar, which is still one of the most dangerous regions of the country. In Operation Athena from 2003 to 2005, our soldiers were right in the capital of Kabul as part of the International Assistance Force.

After NATO took over in Afghanistan, the Defence Department admitted we even had an elite anti-terrorist group running around, conducting operations like something out of an action movie. Forty soldiers of what's known as Joint Task Force 2 (JTF2) were on the job near Kandahar. In *Canada in Afghanistan*, Peter Pigott notes that as part of a U.S. operation against Al Qaeda, the JTF2 strike teams killed at least 115 Taliban and Al Qaeda soldiers and captured 107 senior Taliban leaders. "The Canadian commandos had led a mountain climb to reach a high-altitude observation post in support of Operation Anaconda and for its service, its members were awarded the Presidential Unit Citation."

Just to bring us full circle, if we can hold our own with such macho SAS/Navy Seal stuff, with feats that even earned the recognition of the U.S. government, it is all the more baffling why an idiot like Fox's Greg Gutfeld would sneer that the Canadian military wanted to "run on the beach in gorgeous white Capri pants." You'd think the laziest researcher at Fox would know how to type "Canadian army" into Google.

Especially when some of those Google entries should turn up the fact that six months into the war, in April 2002, four Canadian soldiers were killed and eight others injured when an American F-16 pilot dropped a 225-kilogram bomb on a live-fire night exercise near Kandahar.

If Americans haven't always been appreciative of our contribution, however, some British have. The general that NATO put in charge of southern Afghanistan, Nick

Carter, said in 2009, "There is much that others can learn from what the Canadian Task Force has achieved in the last nine months."

Carter's praise was timely, as Brigadier-General Daniel Menard was taking over as commander of the Canadian-led Joint Task Force Kandahar from Brigadier-General Jonathan Vance. Vance was highly praised by his NATO allies for focusing Canadian efforts on a number of villages in the Dand district; as a result, they saw a drop in insurgent activity during his tenure.

"Canada," said Carter, "had provided a model of how modern counter-insurgency should be prosecuted."

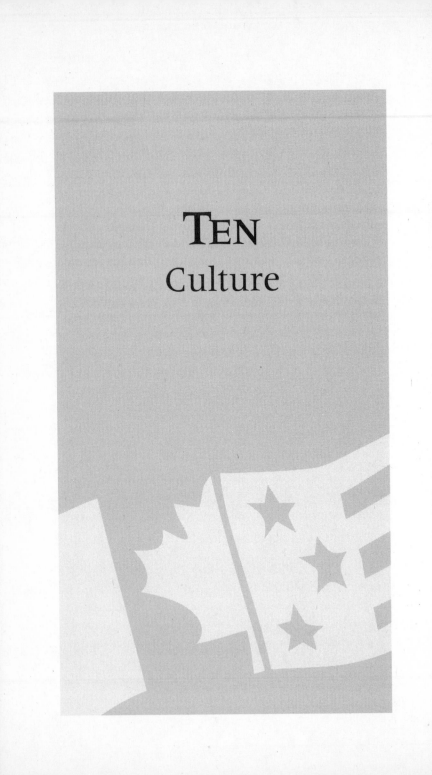

TEN
Culture

NEW AND IMPROVED,
WITHOUT APOLOGIES

IN OUR VAST, COLD LAND, ONCE upon a time there was a dreary period known as the 1970s when culture was something many of us felt we had to apologize for.

The Guess Who, which could boast actual success in the U.S., broke up, and lead singer Burton Cummings devolved into an irritating lounge singer, while for some reason Québec's own answer to a *Tiger Beat* heartthrob was singer René Simard ("René Who?" outside Québec now), who has his own show on Radio Canada these days. We were also punished with such horrible programs as *The King of Kensington* and the excruciatingly unfunny *Wayne & Shuster,* who proved canned laughter could one day get you an Order of Canada. Margaret Atwood was onto her third novel, *Lady Oracle,* in which men are one-dimensional, sexist, misogynistic jerks (for more on the theme of men as one-dimensional sexist, misogynistic jerks, see *Surfacing, Bodily Harm, The Handmaid's Tale* and every other Atwood novel). Mordecai Richler wasn't publishing any novels for a while but was preparing to infuriate Québécois by comparing the PQ to Hitler in *The Atlantic Monthly.* It was a time when Canadian movies got nice, fat funding but were pretty horrible because the money was used, in most cases, for nothing more than a tax dodge.

Then something happened as the 1980s gathered steam. It happened first in music, where we could boast as many one-hit pop wonders with big, spiky hair as the Americans and Brits could, such as Glass Tiger, who sang, "Don't Forget Me When I'm Gone"—and then we promptly did. But we also had singers of more substance like Bryan Adams and Sarah McLachlan. Douglas Coupland came out with the novel *Generation X*, and director Denys Arcand made the film *The Decline of the American Empire*, which wasn't about Americans or an empire, but really about sex. (If they had done the movie in English, yeah, of course, it would sound pretentious, but hey, it's in French, so it *must* be deep!)

We actually began to take pride, not just among ourselves but out in the wider world, for our cultural accomplishments. Then a few of us at last realized we've always had good bits in our culture. Hey, even in the horribly brown, corduroy 1970s, we still had Leonard Cohen to listen to on vinyl (and depress the hell out of us) and Dave Broadfoot to laugh at. (Broadfoot appointed himself as the fictional MP of the New Apathetic Party for Kicking Horse Pass. He once quipped, "When a politician pays $100 a night for a prostitute, he is not a security risk. He's a bad investor.")

No, despite some grim periods, we don't ever have to feel second-place to that great amusement park and popcorn factory to the south. There's stuff we have to work on, and we'll touch on that, but here's how we done good.

Art...or Ahht

This is an easy one. We see the Group of Seven, Tom Thomson and Emily Carr on so many postcards and calendars that we almost take them for granted, but step into a public gallery some time and see the actual canvases themselves, really look at the texture and power of a winter landscape by Lawren Harris or a composition by A.Y. Jackson. At an international exhibition in 1924 in Wembley in the UK, our guys blew the Brits' minds, and then those of the Americans (those with taste) at a later exhibit by the Carnegie Institute.

More recently, we've got cool artists like sculptor Armand Vaillancourt, who yes, is a Québec sovereignty supporter, but we can at least say he was born inside Canada. His fountain, *Québec libre!*, is located in Justin Herman Plaza along The Embarcadero in San Francisco. Not everyone's a fan, and one snotty critic dubbed it, "Stonehenge unhinged with plumbing troubles." But we say screw the critics, because not every artist has U2 spray-painting their work. (Bono wrote "Rock n' Roll stops the traffic" on it.)

The evidence suggests that Vaillancourt approved. Indeed, he wrote the first graffiti on his own sculpture on the eve of its dedication back in 1971. It was assumed that vandals had done the graffiti, so the red paint spelling out "Québec libre" got whitewashed over. Vaillancourt came back, and this time he wrote it in front of witnesses. "It's a joy to make a free statement. This fountain is dedicated to all freedom. Free Québec! Free East Pakistan! Free Vietnam! Free the whole world!"

Then there's Michael Snow, whom the *Village Voice* has always seemed to love and who has walked away with a Guggenheim Fellowship and a Los Angeles Film Critics Association Award. If you don't know his name but have visited Toronto, you've likely seen his work: those geese frozen in mid-flight in the Eaton Centre mall are his, as are the loveable sculpted fans on the sides of the Rogers Centre.

Do we have better artists than America? It's a subjective field, but as we've seen, even American critics like our art.

A Maple Leaf in Every Genre

Where do you want to start? We've got jazz titans like Oscar Peterson, and more recently, Diana Krall. We had a beautiful opera star in Portia White, and we had our own tortured genius of classical, Glenn Gould, who hummed as he played and who—because he dressed in mittens and a coat even in warm weather—got arrested once in Florida as a vagrant while sitting on a bench. We had a country music great in Hank Snow, originally from Nova Scotia, who sang "I've Been Everywhere." For nearly three decades, we've enjoyed the unusual siren talent of k.d. lang (who annoyingly insists we lower-case her like e.e. cummings) and we have our own country music babe, Shania Twain, who recorded the best-selling country album ever recorded by a female artist, *Come on Over*.

From Neil Young to Deborah Cox to the Crash Test Dummies—we could fill whole pages just with the

Canadian Singers/Bands

Musician	Birthplace	Genre
Arcade Fire (William Butler, Win Butler, Régine Chassagne, Jeremy Gara, Tim Kingsbury, Sarah Neufeld, Richard Reed Parry)	Montreal, Quebec	Indie
Paul Brandt	Calgary, Alberta	Country
Michael Bublé	Burnaby, British Columbia	Jazz, Soft Rock
Feist (Leslie Feist)	Amherst, Nova Scotia	Indie
Nelly Furtado	Victoria, British Columbia	Pop
Kardinal Offishall (Jason Harrow)	Toronto, Ontario	Hip hop
k-os (Kevin Brereton)	Toronto, Ontario	Rap/Hip hop
Diana Krall	Nanaimo, British Columbia	Jazz
Jason McCoy	Minesing, Ontario	Country
Nickelback (Daniel Adair, Chad Kroeger, Mike Kroeger, Ryan Peake)	Hanna, Alberta	Rock

names of performers and bands who have achieved international stardom (we could do the same thing with actors, of course). If anything, our rock and pop idols have become so mainstream that Americans even forget these performers are Canadian. The good thing is that the performers don't.

When Alanis Morissette took U.S. citizenship in 2005, she promised, "I will never renounce my Canadian citizenship. I consider myself a Canadian-American."

Television: "We Dinna Have the Power—Oh, Wait, Yeah We Do!"

Eccch. Let's admit it, it is painful. We can't say all of it has been painful, but boy, that sucking sound you hear is a relentless circling of the drain as Canadian TV shows quickly slip into mediocrity. Given a choice between switching on the CBC or an American network (let's face it, if you watch CTV or Global in the evening, you're still watching American TV most of the time), ratings prove you will flee from the MotherCorp.

You want to get nationalistic and defensive? You say our TV never stank? Three words for you: *Front Page Challenge*. Oh, the humanity. Quiz shows and current event-pop culture panels in England and America rotate in different contestants. The CBC preferred to have the same ones all the time. They were all minor celebs who Canadians could watch literally age week after week. From 1957 to 1995! Talk about running a premise into the ground—the CBC was at drilling depth.

But there's a distinction between good Canadian television writers and awful Canadian television. And Canadian TV did do something in the past that, no kidding, changed the world. Nope, we don't mean in the touchy-feely sense of inspiring someone or anything vague like that;

169

we mean it actually, tangibly changed one aspect of our everyday society. More about that in a bit.

The sad part is we have had some exceptional shows to rival American ones, including ones for kids. In fact, it took Canada to appreciate two American geniuses of kids programming. If you're of a certain age, you grew up with these famous words: "Look up. Look *waaaaay* up!" The Friendly Giant, a.k.a. Bob Homme, spoke the words in the program of the same name. He hung out with Rusty, a rooster who played the harp and lived in a sack, and Jerome the giraffe. Oddly enough, the show started on radio in Homme's native Madison, Wisconsin, before the CBC invited the Giant to come move north. *Mr. Dressup*, Ernie Coombs, was from Maine. We loved Coombs and Homme so much that both were inducted into the Order of Canada.

We also had a highly influential and controversial CBC news magazine show in the sixties, *This Hour Has Seven Days* (if you're under 30 reading this, and you always wanted to know where *This Hour Has 22 Minutes* got its name from, now you know). Granted, *Seven Days* ripped off a little of a British show, *That Was the Week That Was*, but it was more journalistic and pioneered the "ambush interview" of politicians and assorted villains. The show had a heck of a premiere—on its first show, it had Lee Harvey Oswald's mother insisting her son was framed (hmmm...) and the Beatles making a splash in Toronto. Of course, it also had its controversies. Co-host Laurier LaPierre once wiped away tears over one story (so much for objective reporting), and on another show, a confrontation was clearly looked for when KKK members were interviewed and a black civil rights activist was brought on set as a surprise guest.

It was an exciting show, groundbreaking—of course the CBC cancelled it. But it was a program that helped inspire *60 Minutes,* which would have as one of its earliest reporters another Canadian, Morley Safer, from Toronto (see page 174).

And here's as good a place as any to come back to how Canadian television changed the world. Back in 1956, future paperback novelist Arthur Hailey dashed off in nine days an hour-long drama script for the CBC called *Flight into Danger.* The plot was simple but compelling: when the pair of pilots for a commercial flight both suffer food poisoning, a passenger, who has never flown a jet before but has been behind the controls of small craft, has to land the plane! Sure, today it's a cliché, but it was riveting to see a pre-"Scotty" James Doohan—yes, without the Scottish accent—try to handle the controls without panicking.

Each time the drama premiered on Canadian, American and British television, network phones lit up right away with enthusiastic calls from viewers who had never seen such a story before and liked what they saw.

And by the way, just as a point of trivia, James Doohan really could fly a plane. A heroic combat officer on the beaches at D-Day, he trained to fly a Taylorcraft Auster prop plane.

Flight into Danger was later made into a feature film for the Americans called *Zero Hour!* (Somebody must have thought the exclamation mark highlighted the danger.)

And that's why every airline in the world doesn't allow its pilots to eat the same meal. Seriously.

Alas, that was one of the few high points for Canadian TV. For the most part, homegrown Canadian dramas have unbelievably sucked, from the when-will-it-please-die *Degrassi* to the clichéd, American-imitation prime-time soaps of *Street Legal* and (ugh) *Wild Roses.* Not to be outdone, CTV has attempted its own viewer

CANADA VS. THE UNITED STATES

lobotomies with fare such as *Whistler*. We're also routinely driven into coma every few years with another
version of *Anne of Green Gables*, which suggests development executives can't or don't want to read any other
good Canadian novels worthy of adaptation, let alone
original scripts. The one notable exception in this tundra,
especially for the CBC, is *The Border*, which not only got
American networks interested in buying it, but it already
airs on several channels in Europe and even Asia.
Co-creator Peter Raymont said of his show, "We think of
it as *24* with a conscience." (For that priceless line alone,
Raymont should go down in Canadian TV history.)

But you can't plunk down and watch a whole night
of good Canadian drama. The product doesn't exist in
enough quantity. Because we're such nice people, and
we like being considered nice people, and because in
our paradise of multiculturalism with same-sex rights
and social justice, you can bet you will never see
a show like *House, M.D.*, in which the sleuth-like hero
is a flawed, bad-tempered, borderline racist and sexist
jerk. Can you imagine the CBC quaking over the hand-
ful of letters from someone bound to be offended?

Now if you recall, I drew a careful distinction between
what airs on our Canadian networks and what Canadian
television writers are doing. Because in the wake of the
U.S. Writers' Guild Strike in 2007-08, the American networks actually turned to us to fill the big, gaping holes in
their program schedules, buying new shows like *Flashpoint*
and the painfully clichéd crime drama, *The Listener*
(a show about a paramedic who reads minds; after a few
episodes, NBC wondered what it was thinking). CBS
joined up with CTV over a brilliant and raw police series
from the keyboard of writer/producer Alan Di Fiore, *The
Bridge*. For what might be the first time, the American
execs in Hollywood and New York weren't just looking at

Canada as a cheap place to shoot; our writers and producers were developing the content.

So when it comes to TV, it's not a who-does-it-better issue. We're actually getting better because of the Americans. Here's hoping the trend continues.

Television Journalism: Wiping Clean Those Star-spangled Glasses

There's no doubt we've tried to keep the Americans honest when it comes to the nightly news for quite a while now, even when they sometimes don't want us to. As with American movies and TV, Canadians have always been there, writing and reporting in broadcast newsrooms. The current list of our expats with mikes could go on and on, from John Roberts now on CBS (whom Canadians used to know as "J.D. Roberts," a co-host of MuchMusic's once-brilliant magazine show, *The New Music*) to Robert MacNeil of the *MacNeil/Lehrer Report* to Keith Morrison and Hilary Brown to MSNBC reporter Donna Friesen, who was a year behind me in the same humble community college journalism course back in Winnipeg.

In the sixties, ABC put Peter Jennings in its anchor slot (replacing another Canadian, by the way), but Americans didn't like his accent and his CBC English, especially when he pronounced "lieutenant" as "leftenant;" it also didn't help that he was a mere 26 years old (and looked 12 in his suit on air). Americans preferred more avuncular, mature anchors. So after three years, Jennings went off to be a foreign correspondent, spending at least seven years in Beirut.

"Peter was one of the first U.S. foreign correspondents to strike a more balanced note on the Israeli-Palestinian issue and to report in depth about Palestinian grievances," CBC reporter David Halton said of him. And Jennings was the first to speak to Ayatollah Khomeini

173

after his return to Iran. By the time ABC wanted him back in the anchor slot, he was a seasoned, urbane vet who looked like journalism's version of James Bond.

According to Halton, American critics sometimes used Jennings' Canadian citizenship against him, and his friends regularly pushed him to become an American. But with 14 Emmys, two Peabody Awards and a life spent more in America than in his native country, Jennings became a U.S. citizen only in 2003, saying he felt closer to Americans in the wake of 9/11. Whenever there was an issue of U.S.-Canada relations or trade, he was quick to point out to his audience how important we are to their economy. "He was passionate about Canadians," said Peter Mansbridge. Playing a crucial role in shaping ABC's coverage, he also gave his American viewers a wider perspective on what was going on beyond their borders. His program was, after all, called *World News Tonight*.

Morley Safer, another Toronto boy, was one of the first TV reporters to point out that something very wrong was going on in Vietnam. In 1965, Safer showed U.S. Marines using a flamethrower and Zippo lighters to torch every hut in the village of Cam Ne, including one that still had people inside in their dugout shelter (it is truly horrifying footage). Lyndon Johnson called up the president of CBS and told him that he had just "shat on the American flag." The next few days, Johnson threatened CBS, demanding it pull Safer out of Vietnam or he would blow the lid on their reporter being "a Communist or KGB agent." The trouble was, Safer wasn't a Communist or an agent; he was just Canadian.

Then there are the Kent brothers, Peter and Arthur, who have both worked for NBC. Arthur Kent became famous as the "Scud Stud" when he reported from a Saudi Arabian rooftop during the 1991 Gulf War. But a few years later, he had an all-out bitter war of his own with

NBC over the way it did stories. For instance, when Kent wanted to explore the economic rebirth of Eastern Europe after the fall of Communism, *Dateline* preferred a racy item on the economics of prostitution and the sex trade. A contract dispute prompted the peacock to try to exile him to Croatia, which at the time was a war zone.

Kent's response was to picket right outside Rockefeller Plaza. They fired him. Kent sued. Guess who won? His settlement meant he pocketed an undisclosed sum of money, plus NBC had to retract certain nasty comments they made about him, and he kept the right to actually publish testimony and evidence from the discovery phase of his lawsuit.

Nor has the feisty reporter, whom his own sister once described as "a little pit bull," seemed to mellow over personal injustices. The makers of the 2007 film *Charlie Wilson's War* merrily helped themselves to Kent's footage from a report on Afghanistan in 1986—without asking him. Back he went to court, saying in a statement: "I brought these actions only to uphold the copyright protection of my work, my voice and my archive, and to make clear that I do not endorse the account of historical events conveyed by the movie." The man does know Afghanistan. He has reported on the country off and on for about 20 years, and his documentary for PBS in 2001 on life under the Taliban got raves from the critics.

He reached a settlement with Universal Studios under terms that left him "very pleased."

More recently, there's the example of Bob McKeown, who has worked for NBC and CBS but has made an interesting exploration of American media after coming back to the CBC. McKeown, by the way, has to be the only guy who has ever won not only two Emmys but also a Grey Cup (he used to be an all-star centre with the

Ottawa Roughriders). He also has the dubious distinction of getting punched by *Wild Kingdom* host Marlin Perkins, after he asked the zoologist about faking footage of animals (which Perkins regularly did—one of the most infamous cases was when he dropped a bunch of lemmings into a river to suggest they committed mass suicide). In 2005, McKeown took on right-wing loon Ann Coulter when he disputed her casual rewrite of history in claiming Canada sent troops to Vietnam (see what we really did on page 156). McKeown exemplified our "softer" approach to journalism when he challenged her on *The Fifth Estate* over her vilifying of American liberals.

"They are the enemy," insisted Coulter, who claimed liberals were rooting against their own country.

"Simply because they don't see things your way?" asked McKeown reasonably.

McKeown also examined Bill "Shut Up" O'Reilly of the Fox News Network, who while interviewing Canadian newspaper columnist Heather Mallick made a grandiose and ridiculous threat of launching an economic boycott against Canada (one that never happened). After *The Fifth Estate* aired its piece, O'Reilly—who refused to grant McKeown an interview—vaguely compared him to Nazi propagandists.

In keeping with the spirit of "fair and balanced" reporting (as Fox insists it does), the alleged propagandists at the CBC offered a link to O'Reilly's response on its own website.

We're No Friends of Fox

Given that McKeown was digging into how the media in the U.S. got saddled with labels of "liberal" and "conservative," it's interesting to note how American and Canadian media have always been essentially different.

Even back when the *New York Times* ruled and Dan Rather had a seventies haircut and wore cowboy boots in Southeast Asia, American reporters often looked at the world in terms of how a story overseas affected the U.S. What, if any, role did the U.S. have to play and what was it doing about it? What was a country's reaction to how much or how little the U.S. cared about the problem? The idea that a foreign country might have bigger things on its mind than worrying what the U.S. thought was ignored. If networks didn't care about another country's culture or the war zone was too hot, well...a Canadian was usually willing to go.

But in spite of the occasional tunnel vision, many American reporters were genuinely interested back then in getting the objective facts. Many today still are, of course, but when Bill Moyers, one of the typewriter titans from an age of arguably more open dissent, chose to retire in 2004, he said, "We have an ideological press that's interested in the election of Republicans, and a mainstream press that's interested in the bottom line. Therefore, we don't have a vigilant, independent press whose interest is the American people."

Are we any better? Mostly yes. True, there are regular instances of bias and the so-called bottom line in our print and broadcast journalism, as well as a downright appalling lack of competition. The editor-in-chief of *Maclean's*, for instance, is Ken Whyte, who used to edit the now-defunct, conservative *Alberta Report*; before him, it was Matthew Fraser, who was editor-in-chief at Conrad Black's *National Post*. The media in Canada is a nice, small club, especially on the corporate side. CTVglobemedia, for example, owns CTV Television, CHUM Radio, and the *Globe and Mail*, plus it holds a 20 percent stake in TorStar, which is a neat trick, because the *Toronto Star* is the *Globe*'s major competition in the biggest city in Canada. We'd alert the CRTC, but look how cute it is over there sleeping in the corner, sucking its thumb....

Despite those gripes above, our media is still carrying the torch of objectivity and critical investigation. Canadian broadcast news, after all, for better or for worse, grew out of the BBC model (although, fortunately, we didn't carry the absurd practice of having radio announcers on the CBC give the news in black tie). We're interested in the world, and when we fly over, we often try to see it from the point of view of the people who live there. We have our 24-hour news networks, but we'd be horrified if we were offered one with an openly partisan approach to covering events, like Fox.

As it is, Fox News regularly picks a quarrel with Canada. Apparently, we're a terrifying threat. We have universal health care and gay marriage, we didn't support the

Main Media (newspapers, tv stations, radio stations)

Parent Company	Some Major Media Holdings
CTVglobemedia	CTV Television Network, A Channel, CP24, Bravo, Comedy Network, TSN, CHUM Radio, Globe and Mail
Rogers Communications	Citytv, Omni Television, Sportsnet, The Shopping Channel, Maclean's, Chatelaine, Flare, MoneySense, Today's Parent
TorStar Corporation	Toronto Star, Metroland, Harlequin Enterprises, 50% of Workopolis, a 20% stake in Black Press, and it owns a 20% stake in CTVglobemedia
Quebecor	Sun Media newspapers, Osprey Media newspapers, 24 Hours commuter papers, TVA Group, Les Éditions Quebecor, Les Éditions Libre Expression
Canwest Global	Global Television, Showcase Network, BBC Canada, National Post, Calgary Herald, Regina Leader-Post, Vancouver Sun

war in Iraq, and yet somehow we haven't imploded; just our very existence undermines all their fear-mongering. Unfortunately, we have to take note of what they do because they average 2.2 million viewers, and their audience has been growing. Buuuuuuut...Fox likes to shoot itself in the foot. Regularly. It can be quite entertaining.

Like most liars, it engages in really foolish lies. For one of its reports on free speech in Canada related to criticism of Muslims, Fox interviewed an individual it identified as a "free speech activist"—the problem was the "activist" was a neo-Nazi hate-monger who has ties to racist skinhead organizations in Ontario and Alberta! Then there's the example of its insulting ignorance of our Afghanistan contribution (see page 160).

Even when Fox covers its own news at home, it still refuses to get it right. In November 2009, it carried a story supposedly covering a huge rally against health care reform in Washington. On the *Daily Show*, host Jon Stewart took great pleasure in unmasking Fox's blatant inclusion of archive footage from a better-attended rally back in September—the trees were still green, the sky noticeably cloudier and people dressed differently for the weather.

"Although it pains me to say this," Fox News host Sean Hannity declared the next night, "Jon Stewart, Comedy Central—he was right." Hannity claimed the use of the footage was an "inadvertent mistake." This beggars belief, because anyone who has ever worked in a TV newsroom knows you physically store archive footage in a different place than the visuals you've shot for events that day—even if it's digital.

There are still newsrooms where if you pulled a stunt like this, you'd be instantly fired. But not at Fox.

Many observers have praised Stewart and the *Daily Show* for turning a critical eye on the U.S. media and breaking stories that the mainstream media itself hadn't looked into. Fox is a favourite target, but Stewart also skewered the overblown, misleading hype of CNBC's Wall Street coverage during the 2008 economic meltdown.

And helping him with his comic crusade are two Canadians, Samantha Bee and Jason Jones.

Movies

We rock when it comes to movies. Okay, yes, if we put our movies side by side with American ones, it would be embarrassing. We can't match them for output, not that anyone's trying. (And quite frankly, Bollywood beats the Yanks hands down for endless production— in the time that you've read this paragraph, they've already written a script, shot footage and are editing a new movie.) Nor do we measure up in terms of quality or box office.

Yes, there, we've said it. And don't kid yourself with any defensive nationalism—the highest grossing Canadian film internationally of all time is still...sigh, *Porky's*, the granddaddy of all insipid teen sex romps. And it wasn't even directed or written by a Canadian or even shot here, it was simply funded with Canadian money!

Exhibit B for the prosecution would likely be Paul Gross turning the battle of Passchendaele in World War One into the fat, expensive, government-funded *Passionlessdale*, a film in which the heroine actually mouths cringe-inducing dialogue such as, "There's only one rule: don't die." ("Sure, hon, instead I'll get an arm blown off, or my legs, or perhaps I'll get blinded by mustard gas....")

Movies and tv series filmed in Canada that are set in the U.S.

Title	Location Where Story is Set	Location Where Several Scenes or All of Film Actually Made
Rumble in the Bronx	New York	Vancouver
The Time Traveler's Wife	Chicago	Toronto, Hamilton
X-Men	New York	Toronto, Hamilton, Oshawa
X-2	New York, "Alkali Lake" in Canada yet has U.S. military guys running around our sovereign territory	Winnipeg, Burlington, Toronto, Vancouver, Kannaskis Country, Alberta, Royal Roads, Colwood, B.C.
Good Will Hunting	Boston	Toronto
Chicago	Chicago	Toronto
The Long Kiss Goodnight	Honesdale, Pennsylvania and a Niagara Falls without any RCMP or Canadian border guards	Toronto, Hamilton, Muskoka, Niagara Falls
Traitor	Various, including Halifax and Chicago	Toronto, Hamilton
Shall We Dance?	Chicago	Winnipeg
Battlestar Galactica	Space	Vancouver
Smallville	Kansas	Vancouver

181

When we go by what we supposedly make for ourselves, yes, we've had exceptions like Denys Arcand and Sarah Polley—but we mostly get dreck. The truth is, we make good movies when we go to the Land of Opportunity.

We don't have to compare Canada versus the U.S. because we are already in the American movie industry in so many ways. And we have been for quite some time.

Everyone knows how we stand in for America as a backdrop.

Winnipeg worked for Chicago in the American remake of *Shall We Dance?*, and the Prairies stepped in for Kansas in *Capote*. Jackie Chan even tried to persuade everybody that Vancouver could pass for New York in *Rumble in the Bronx*, which has to be a quite a suspension of disbelief—you can see the Coast Mountains right in the background of some shots.

I heard a tale that I did my best to find attribution for, about the movie adaptation of the Scott Pilgrim comic book series, *Scott Pilgrim vs. the World*, that falls under the category of "If it ain't true, it ought to be." The movie, just as the comic book, is set in Canada, right in our biggest city, with all its landmarks proudly on show, but the story goes that allegedly when the Canadian dollar soared above the greenback in 2008, the producers actually considered getting New York to stand in for Toronto! Now wouldn't that be a nice switch?

As much as Hollywood brings money and jobs up north when they shoot here, there's still a fair bit of grumbling since most often it's the production work we're getting—the lift that bail, tote that light—rather than seeing ourselves or having our own stories told. But if you judge an industry by the people involved in it, Hollywood really is ours. Consider the following tidbits:

- King Kong was crazy for a gal born on a ranch in Cardston, Alberta: Fay Wray. "America's sweetheart" Mary Pickford was from Toronto. Mack Sennett, the director of the Keystone Cops silent movies, was an Irish Catholic boy from Québec. Jack Warner of Warner Bros came from London, Ontario, while Louis B. Mayer of MGM spent years living in Saint John, New Brunswick (but we don't brag too much about either of them, since they were both real bastards; Warner favoured blacklisting, and Mayer called Judy Garland a "hunchback" and gave her pep pills).

- Today, there's Paul Haggis from London, Ontario, who tapped out the scripts for *Million Dollar Baby* and *Crash,* two big Oscar winners, and then helped reboot the James Bond franchise as a co-writer of *Casino Royale* and *Quantum of Solace* (when a Canadian female agent walks out the door in a crucial final scene of *Quantum* and mumbles, "Thank you," you just know those perfect manners had to come from the Haggis keyboard).

- We have director James Cameron, who gave us not only scary *Aliens* but also scary robots (the *Terminator* franchise) and then went on to put us all on a scary ship, *Titanic* (the sinking isn't so scary, it's the theme music sung by Céline Dion). More recently, he has made scary American soldiers versus nicer blue aliens (*Avatar*).

- Although he doesn't spend much time here anymore, we still claim Ivan Reitman, who grew up in Toronto and is a graduate of Hamilton's McMaster University, and who has produced some of the biggest movie hits ever, such as *Animal House* and *Ghostbusters.* His son, Jason, born in Montréal, is now a successful director in his own right with *Thank You for Smoking*.

- We still have Norman Jewison, a Canadian Jewish kid from Toronto, who held up a brilliant mirror to blacks and whites in the American south when he directed the film version of *In the Heat of the Night*. Then he went on to direct film classics such as *Fiddler on the Roof* and *Jesus Christ Superstar*.

- If you want creepy mixed with provocative (or pretentious, depending on your tastes), there's always David Cronenberg, who has had guns swimming around the stomach of James Woods (*Videodrome*) and who turned Jeff Goldblum into *The Fly* before he made *Eastern Promises*.

- Or you can go see the work of Atom Egoyan, a long-time darling of Cannes judges, or the...well, let's call it the *challenging* work of Guy Maddin, who actually got Isabella Rossellini to come to Winnipeg for *The Saddest Music in the World*.

Actors? We could fill pages with their names, from the incomparable Hume Cronyn (another London, Ontario, native) to Brendan Fraser to Christopher Plummer to Donald Sutherland and son Kiefer. Leslie Nielsen was a straight man for the fifties classic *Forbidden Planet* before he reached his real fame with *Naked Gun* and *Airplane*. (And don't call him Shirley). Then there are funnymen Dan Akroyd, Eugene Levy, John Candy, Mike Myers and Jim Carrey.

There are the beautiful acting goddesses Kim Cattral and the under-appreciated Genevieve Bujold, plus Kate Nelligan, who has racked up so many nominations and wins for Oscar, Tony, Emmy, BAFTA awards—and even the Laurence Olivier Award—that it's easy to lose track.

Canadian Actors

Actor	Birthplace	Date of Birth	Select Filmography
Hayden Christensen	Vancouver, British Columbia	April 19, 1981	*Jumper; Shattered Glass; Star Wars: Episode II—Attack of the Clones*
Ryan Gosling	London, Ontario	November 12, 1980	*Breaker High (TV); The Notebook; Stay*
Evangeline Lilly	Fort Saskatchewan, Alberta	August 3, 1979	*The Hurt Locker; The Long Weekend; Lost (TV)*
Rachel McAdams	London, Ontario	November 17, 1978	*Mean Girls; The Notebook; The Time Traveller's Wife*
Brendan Fehr	New Westminster, British Columbia	October 29, 1977	*CSI: Miami (TV); The Other Side of the Tracks; Roswell (TV)*
Ryan Reynolds	Vancouver, British Columbia	October 23, 1976	*Blade: Trinity; Definitely, Maybe; The Proposal*
Neve Campbell	Guelph, Ontario	October 3, 1973	*Partition; Party of Five (TV); Scream*
Carrie Anne Moss	Vancouver, British Columbia	August 21, 1967	*Love Hurts; The Matrix; Memento*
Eugene Levy	Hamilton, Ontario	December 17, 1946	*American Pie; Cheaper by the Dozen 2; SCTV (TV)*
Christopher Plummer	Toronto, Ontario	December 13, 1939	*The Imaginarium of Doctor Parnassus; Up; The Lake House; The Sound of Music*

And we have Sarah Polley, who while still under 30 directed a titan like Julie Christie in *Away From Her*, and who, incidentally, knows how to tell American executives when to get stuffed. Disney was carrying Polley's show *Road to Avonlea* on its channel when its management asked her—more like strongly insisted—she not wear a peace symbol necklace at an awards show while the Gulf War was going on; she said no. We say good for her.

We have arguably the greatest ham of all time, William Shatner (born in Montréal), and we had another Canadian in the far future, James Doohan, whose life and career was fascinating even before he played "Scotty" on *Star Trek*. (He once slalomed a plane through two mountain telegraph poles to prove it could be done).

And dude, we have, like, two stars of *The Matrix*— Keanu Reeves (grew up in Toronto) and Carrie-Anne Moss (born in Burnaby, BC). Whoa!

Be Proud of Our Genre Trash!

When it comes to books, we're well stacked against American letters or those of many other countries. Naturally, most people will first think of our "literary fiction" authors, such as Atwood, Michael Ondaatje or Pulitzer Prize-winning Carol Shields. None of them need more publicity, and frankly, we have a lot more to be proud of by the breadth and scope of our books than just the middle-class authors of "literary fiction" (an oxymoronic term that implies what the rest of us do amounts to finger-painting). It's in this way that we surprisingly measure up quite well against the U.S., and it's high time we realized it. But before we hit the paperbacks....

You want the romanticism of expat bohemians in Paris? We got 'em. There's Morley Callaghan, sadly not read as much these days, who was in Paris with the same Lost Generation and who beat Hemingway badly at boxing (Hemingway, the big bully egomaniac, promptly blamed Scott Fitzgerald for not using the stopwatch

Canadian Writers

Name	Genre	Titles	Birthplace
Kate Bridges	Romance	*The Surgeon, Frontier Christmas, Alaska Bride on the Run*	Kirkland Lake, Ontario
Julianne Maclean	Romance	*The Mistress Diaries, When a Stranger Loves Me*	Halifax, Nova Scotia
Lyn Hamilton	Mysteries	Lara McClintoch series	Toronto, Ontario
William Deverell	Mysteries	*Snow Job, Mind Games, Kill All the Lawyers*	Regina, Saskatchewan
Joy Fielding	Thrillers	*Still Life, Kiss Mommy Goodbye, See Jane Run*	Toronto, Ontario
Robert J. Sawyer	Science Fiction	*Flashforward, Hominids, The Terminal Experiment*	Ottawa, Ontario
Tanya Huff	Science Fiction/ Fantasy	the *Blood* Books, *Valor* series	Halifax, Nova Scotia
Guy Gavriel Kay	Science Fiction/ Fantasy	*Tiganna, The Fionavar Tapestry*	Weyburn, Saskatchewan

properly to time the rounds). We have John Glassco, who wrote the classic *Memoirs of Montparnasse*. And we have the incomparable Mavis Gallant, who penned countless short stories for *The New Yorker*.

Americans have Laura Ingalls Wilder in a little house on the prairie. We have that redheaded kid. You know, what's her name...hangs around gables. Loved the world over, especially by Japanese tourists.

The biggest romance publishing company in the world—Harlequin—actually started in, of all places,

Winnipeg. Thanks to a handshake deal at the Ritz Hotel in London, England, Harlequin was allowed to reprint Mills & Boon romance novels. (It rejected some that were a little too racy, believe it or not, and think about that for a moment—English novels racier than Canadian ones!) Eventually, they took over the British company in 1971. They're worldwide today, an absolutely huge enterprise, based now in Don Mills.

Oh, you don't read trashy romances? What about mysteries? Science fiction? We have them. And the rest of the world knows about us when it comes to genre fiction; we just don't know ourselves.

William Deverell used to be one of Vancouver's top criminal lawyers. Then he turned mystery writer and racked up a Dashiell Hammett award along the way. In 2009, in the *National Post*, Deverell blasted the literary snobbery that is perpetrated by the country's big publishing houses, libraries, universities, the arts councils and the CBC. During a BC arts festival workshop, Deverell "was instructed by a Canada Council spokeswoman, in severe tones, that it does not support writers of crime fiction." Deverell lamented how "the Brits knight their genre writers, the Yanks lionize them, but the Canucks (or at least our persons of letters) continue to treat them like unwashed in-laws tracking mud into the parlour. So sad."

Deverell isn't alone in a scathing view of Canada's literary establishment. On his *New York Times* blog, Douglas Coupland witheringly described CanLit as "when the Canadian government pays you money to write about life in small towns and/or the immigration experience." Watching a broadcast of the Giller Prize awards, Coupland wrote, "It was as if I'd tuned into the Monster Mash—not a soul under 60, and I could practically smell the mummy dust in the room." Canada's biggest publishing secret is its wealth of genre writers who can match any paperback on the shelves of a Barnes and Noble in Seattle.

Consider Deverell's field of mysteries and thrillers. Canadian-born Susanna Kearsley, a former museum curator, has had her novels translated into other languages and optioned for films, plus she won the UK's Catherine Cookson Fiction Prize in 1993. Lyn Hamilton's antique dealer sleuth, Lara McClintoch, chased clues through 11 books before the author died of cancer in 2009. Her novels were also translated into other languages, and the fourth in the McClintoch series formed the basis of a 2003 *Murder She Wrote* TV movie. There's Joy Fielding, who would have plenty to write about even if she didn't choose thrillers—she once acted in an episode of *Gunsmoke* and got a kiss from Elvis Presley. Her novels, which include *See Jane Run* and *Whispers and Lies,* have made the *New York Times* bestseller list. And although Peter Robinson is an import, he has lived in Canada for decades, having his famous Detective Chief Inspector Alan Banks solve crimes in Yorkshire, all from the comfort of his home in The Beaches district of Toronto.

Canadians can especially hold our own when it comes to science fiction and fantasy. One of the greats of the SF Golden Age, A.E. van Vogt, who wrote the classic, *Slan,* comes from Manitoba and used to work for the Defence Department. We have Guy Gavriel Kay, born in Weyburn, Saskatchewan, and raised in Winnipeg, who can get you wonderfully lost in the fictional realm of Sarantium.

Bakka-Phoenix Books on Toronto's quirky Queen Street should be made into a city landmark, it has employed so many names in science fiction: Michelle Sagara, Tanya Huff (whose series featuring detective Vicki Nelson was turned into the short-lived but cult favourite TV show, *Blood Ties*) and Robert J. Sawyer (who has won the two biggest awards in SF, a Hugo and a Nebula). One of Sawyer's novels inspired the TV series *FlashForward*. (And yet the Canada Council's peer assessors actually turned down Sawyer for residency at Yukon's Berton House!)

Just because these authors write science fiction doesn't mean their books cop out of being Canadian. Huff's *Blood* novel series is set in Toronto. Sawyer's books can be unapologetically filled with Canuck references; in *Calculating God*, an alien lands outside Toronto's Royal Ontario Museum and demands, "Take me to a palaeontologist."

And we have transplanted Americans whose SF careers arguably took off only when they came to Canada. There's William Gibson, who came north to evade the Vietnam War draft and who practically invented the cyberpunk genre with *Neuromancer*. There's also Spider Robinson, known for his humour and for inventing the SF landmark Callahan's Place, who has divided his years here between British Columbia and Nova Scotia.

And then there's Judith Merrill, who left the U.S. over politics in the 1960s and who later donated a wealth of books and magazines she owned to a Toronto library. Merrill was also good at deflating Canadian pomposity. One time when the Writers' Union of Canada—already getting full of itself—debated whether writers "could" write about opposite genders and other ethnic groups, she piped up, "Who will speak for the aliens?" That ended that nonsense.

Those American SF writers who have chosen to stay on Planet Canada would no doubt admit they have the best of both worlds, having done some of their best work here.

ELEVEN
Crime and Punishment

MORE GANGS
THAN GUNS

AMERICA HAD THE WILD WEST; we had solitary Mounties patrolling huge stretches of prairies and able to put down riots all by themselves. America had Prohibition and gangsters like Al Capone; Canadians were, let's say, more involved in the "supply side" of illegal liquor, with bootlegging runs. The U.S. has had four presidents assassinated: Abe Lincoln, James Garfield, William McKinley and John F. Kennedy, and attempts have been made on every president since Nixon up to George W. Bush. Canada's had only one major federal politician assassinated, and that was D'Arcy McGee when he was shot dead at his doorstep in 1868 by someone who was likely an Irish radical.

The security and the occasionally grim atmosphere of potential doom at the White House and on Air Force One have provided ample fuel for those Hollywood thrillers with stars like Harrison "Get off my plane" Ford. The breaches in Canadian state circles, on the other hand, sometimes have had an almost British comedy atmosphere. (Remember when a guy managed to sneak into Buckingham Palace and the Queen's bedroom?) Think back to when a schizophrenic man armed with a knife managed to break into 24 Sussex Drive in 1995. Jean Chretien's wife, Aline, promptly locked the bedroom door and called for help while our prime minister brandished an Inuit stone sculpture, just in case. It took the Mounties seven minutes to come to their rescue. Maybe their tardiness is why when a protestor got too close in 1996, the prime minister actually used a chokehold on him and pushed him out of the

192

way...all while the Mounties looked on. The media quickly dubbed it the "Shawinigan Handshake."

Sadly, we have our own shameful roster of home-grown serial killers that can easily take their place with the likes of Charles Manson and Jeffrey Dahmer: Clifford Olson, who murdered 11 children in BC, Robert Pickton, recently convicted of the second-degree murders of six women in BC (and charged with the deaths of 20 more), and the sadistic Scarborough rapist Paul Bernardo, who killed three teenage girls with the help of his wife, Karla Holmolka, and whose videos of his depravity haunted his jury.

On the more pleasant side, while Americans have made folk heroes of violent bank robbers like John Dillinger and Bonnie and Clyde, we've occasionally had the prototypically "nice" bank robber. Take the Flying Bandit, Ken Leishman. He was known for his polite, non-violent stickups. Having become a pilot after his stint as a guest of Manitoba's Stony Mountain Penitentiary, Leishman figured out that shipments of gold bullion regularly went through Winnipeg's airport on their way to the mint in Ottawa. So in 1966, he and four other pals in ground crew uniforms took possession of a gold shipment right on the tarmac as if they were conducting ordinary business. They loaded it into a stolen Air Canada van and drove off with almost $400,000 in bullion! After jail time and daring escapes, including one by plane across the U.S. border, Leishman eventually settled down...and wound up as the president of the chamber of commerce and the mayor in Red Lake, Ontario. He died in a plane accident in 1980.

Psychopaths and polite armed robbers aside, we're still a safer country to live in than the United States. Both our countries have had their crimes rate decrease over the last few years, but consider the following facts.

In 2008, according to the FBI, there were 14,180 murders in the U.S.—at least ones that law enforcement agencies knew about. "Of the homicides for which the type of weapon was specified, 71.9 percent involved the use of firearms," reports the FBI blandly. "Of the identified firearms used, handguns comprised 88.3 percent."

In contrast, Canada, with more than 30 million people, had 611 murders in 2008. That was 17 more than the year before, with 200 homicides committed using a firearm. Gun murders have gone up by 24 percent since 2002. You can blame America for the increase—most of our firearms come from there.

2008 Crime Stats

Crime	Canada	United States
Homicide	611	16,272
Aggravated Assault/Assault with a Weapon	58,000	834,885
Robbery	32,000	441,855
Vehicle Theft	125,000	956,846
Impaired Driving Causing Death	193	11,773

A 2009 study for the *Journal of Criminology and Criminal Justice* discovered that two-thirds of crime guns seized in Canada come from the United States. Since one of the study's authors is a gun-control advocate, you might be suspicious of that figure. But in 2006, the Toronto police traced back 120 out of 181 guns used in crimes in our biggest city to the U.S.

That illegal guns come from the U.S. may be no surprise, but StatsCan has a more interesting figure about the nature of our increasing homicides. It says gang-related murders accounted for almost one in four of the homicides in 2008, and they've been on the rise since the 1990s. Sure, America has more gun crime, but an argument can be made that we have an equally bad problem now with gangs.

Canada, believe it or not, has more Hells Angels than any other country, and that includes the United States, the place where they started! Canadian law enforcement authorities say that's because criminal gangs like the Hells Angels have until recently been taking advantage of our lax laws, whereas the U.S. has the Racketeer Influenced and Corrupt Organizations Act, commonly known as RICO, to go after organized crime. But the Harper government introduced new legislation in 2009 to amend the Criminal Code, enacting harsher punishments for violent crimes like drive-by shootings.

And as long as we're on the subject of punishment, Canada has a prison population of more than 38,000. The U.S., in contrast, has more than 2,000,000 people behind bars, the highest incarcerated population in the world.

SMOKE WITHOUT
MIRRORS

ONE OF THE THINGS THAT divides the U.S. from Canada is a long trail of smoke—as in pot smoke. In 2003, Canada became the first country in the world to allow marijuana for medical use. The Netherlands took the step the same year, but the Dutch have the unique luxury of being able to walk into a pharmacy to buy their medical cannabis, unlike Canadians, who need to apply to Health Canada before they can grow their own supply or buy it from a government-authorized grower. Meanwhile, in 2005, the U.S. Supreme Court struck down a state law that would have allowed doctors to prescribe marijuana.

In 2004, the Canadian Medical Association estimated that 1.5 million of us smoke marijuana recreationally, while the Canadian Addiction Survey reported that 14 percent of Canadians said they had used cannabis in the past year. Back in 2000, more than 30,000 Canadians were charged with simple pot possession, according to the Senate Committee on Illegal Drugs. When the committee released its final report in late 2002, it said that marijuana is less harmful than alcohol and should fall under the same sort of regulations.

What about harder drugs? Those drugs that incidentally, the committee says that pot won't lead to. Cocaine and heroin use for Canadians was up in the 1980s and '90s, but usage has steadily declined in recent years, while crystal meth and ecstasy consumption have gone up. There are 50 to 100,000 injection drug users in Canada, a cause for concern when you remember that just in 1996, it was estimated that

3000 out of the 5000 new cases of HIV were probably related to needle use, and today, about 90 percent of hepatitis C infections can be chalked up to it.

In 2003, Vancouver saw the opening of Insite, North America's first legally supervised injection site—a pilot project thanks to Health Canada granting Vancouver Coastal Health an exemption from the Controlled Drugs and Substances Act and ponying up $1.5 million in funding. John Walters, the White House's "drug czar" (director of the Office of National Drug Control Policy) at the time, said harm reduction sites would just encourage heroin use. Vancouver mayor Larry Campbell begged to differ. He countered that Americans should look at their law enforcement and prison system to see if they were winning the drug war. "It's an unmitigated disaster, and they know it, but they can't back out of it."

The same year the harm reduction site was setting up shop in Vancouver, it was estimated 97 million Americans had given pot a try and 15 million had a toke at least monthly (but that's still only 5 percent of the population, considering the U.S. has about 300 million people). In 2005, however, a study by the American Enterprise Institute reported that the number of Americans imprisoned for drug offences had increased from 50,000 in 1980 to 450,000 in 2003. As David T. Jones and David Kilgour wrote in *Uneasy Neighbors: Canada, the USA and the Dynamics of State, Industry and Culture*, "Those figures do not suggest that fear of 'doing the time' has deterred drug dealers or users from doing the crime."

Canadian public attitudes seem to reflect the nuances of the drug landscape. A poll by Angus Reid suggested in early 2009 that 49 percent of us think there's a national drug abuse problem, though 34 percent say it's confined to specific areas and people. And while half of us support legalizing pot, less than eight percent would lift the penalties for drugs such as cocaine and crystal meth. Moreover, three out of four Canadians liked the idea of mandatory minimum prison sentences and hefty fines for grow operators and dealers.

If Americans ever accuse us of being the major pipeline for pot into their country...they're right. In the same vein, the U.S. is responsible for handguns coming north and for being a major stopover in the drug trade that brings Colombian cocaine into our country. A lot of this two-way traffic goes through British Columbia, where "BC bud," as it's called, is a crop that's estimated to be worth up to $10 billion per year and is likely the province's third largest industry. The province's UN gang (so called because of the multi-ethnic flavour of its members) spent $350,000 on two planes to bring in drugs, while officers followed a paper trail that implicated the gang's founder, Clayton Roueche, for $1 million in transactions.

With that kind of windfall for dealers at stake, the violence has also escalated, with everything from machine gunfire to victims of gangs getting tortured, and one man was even found shackled to a basement wall. "What we have seen are new rules of engagement for the gangsters," Vancouver Police Chief Jim Chu told reporters. "They are now shooting each other when they don't have to."

Back to Weeds

Over the years, bills to fully legalize marijuana have been introduced in Canada's Parliament, but politics and current events have gotten in the way, and the Harper government has refused to revive Liberal reform efforts over cannabis, even if many Canadians would like to see pot made legal. Under a Liberal-drafted bill, adults caught with less than 15 grams of marijuana could have been fined up to $400 but wouldn't have received a criminal record; at the same time, the bill would have doubled the length of prison sentences for growers and introduced four new offences for growers. That, of course, dovetails neatly with the latest survey figures suggesting Canadians would prefer to punish dealers and not users.

After Harper announced his government would shelve the draft bill, Alan Young, a law professor at York University and a marijuana-legalization activist, told CTV Newsnet, "I think there's enormous pressure from the United States, and I think Stephen Harper wants to mend fences with George Bush and is quite willing to give up this issue."

Until the law changes, possession of marijuana of up to 30 grams, or hashish of up to one gram, can get you six months, a $1000 fine or both in Canada. In the U.S., according to the Drug Enforcement Agency's own website, "The penalty for possession of marijuana as a misdemeanour can result in a maximum of one year in jail and a $2000 fine...The possession of marijuana as a felony can result in a penalty of a prison sentence of one year and a day to 10 years and a maximum fine of $5000."

Even though the penalties are different, the Harper Conservative government agrees on one thing with the Obama Democratic administration when it comes to pot. Obama's drug czar, Gil Kerlikowske, has flatly declared, "Legalization is not in the president's vocabulary, and it's not in mine." But Kerlikowske also claims, "Marijuana is dangerous and has no medicinal benefit."

As you might expect, law enforcement officers across Canada also don't think legalization is the answer, but surprise—their argument most of the time has nothing to do with whether pot is "harmful" or if it has medicinal benefits for say, cancer patients. They don't like who is doing most of the selling.

"The key is the violence, the overt, physical, public violence that we see," says Sergeant Shinder Kirk of BC's Integrated Gang Task Force, who argues there's always blood on the product at some point on its way to users' hands. The head of the Biker Enforcement Unit for the Ontario Provincial Police, Len Isnor, insists that most of the drugs children are using in schools come from the Hells Angels. And several top cops will tell you that if pot were legalized, the criminals would merely turn to something else.

If Canada ever does legalize pot, you won't hear applause from those behind grow-ops or big drug traffickers, and their grudge would be because of our, well...innate Canadianness. Consider how Britain's newspaper *The Independent* put the legalization case when it profiled Vancouver's drug war in 2009:

> In the long run, many British Columbians, on both left and right, accept that legalisation and regulation are the answer. Just the sales tax on $7 billion of drugs would pay for several hospitals and schools, policing costs could be reduced, property crime by addicts to pay for their drug habits would be slashed, and the gang wars could be quickly reined in.

Yes, all these lovely things could happen. But drug dealers don't want to pay sales tax. And what dealer wants Health Canada and Environment Canada (let alone Revenue Canada), looking over his shoulder, making sure the product is grown with every consideration, no matter what the overhead cost, to the safety of the product and in an environmentally friendly manner? If we're a welfare state, we'll still be a welfare state when it comes to the ganga. And no drug dealer hoping to sit on a mountain of cash in his Gulfstream jet wants that.

TWELVE
International Reputation

SOMETIMES SAVING
EAGLES, SOMETIMES DEALING WITH TURKEYS

IN 2004, AN ONLINE COMPANY, T-shirtKing.com, began selling a "Go Canadian" package—complete with a Canadian flag T-shirt, a Canadian flag lapel pin and, naturally, the cliché patch for the backpack. It even offered a quick reference guide for paranoid Americans on how to speak Canadian and fool the locals of a European country more effectively.

"It's not meant as a slight against the United States or Canada," the company's president insisted to the Associated Press. "It was meant as something Republicans could give their Democrat friends to say, *'C'est la vie.'*...But maybe not *c'est la vie* because that's a French word."

Right, French—that wouldn't be one of our two official languages, would it? You may want to revise that reference guide on Canadians.

Of course, for at least three decades Americans have used the maple leaf as a fig leaf in the hopes they won't be sniffed out as U.S. citizens (and we don't have the heart to tell them, "pssst, guys, you ain't pulling it off"). Whether Europeans—or citizens elsewhere—hate American travellers will always come down to who you talk to among the locals on the backpack trail in the Pyrenees or in the Tuscan countryside. It's purely anecdotal.

But we can weigh the things we've done that have made the world love us (and we love it right back). In Paris, of course, French hotel concierges don't love either Americans or Canadians; they love Visa, MasterCard and Discover.

As for the American record, check out (Anti-)American History, page 113, for a clue to how the world has felt lately about the U.S. and why. You can also see the difference between their style and ours when you check out what America tells its high school and university kids. In the popular textbook, *American Government*, Walter E. Volkomer writes: "Some observers view the president as not only the chief diplomat of the United States but also the leader of the democratic world. This role may be looked upon as an extension of the president's constitutional powers as chief of state, commander in chief and chief diplomat."

Oh, really? That's an amazingly long extension cord. Then in a breathtaking leap of presumption, he writes, "Today no other nation's chief executive can claim to speak with the same authority as the president of the United States." It's the kind of statement that would prompt most professors to scribble in your essay's margin, *"Prove."*

If Americans want to claim authority (usually with a big missile), we prefer to put our flag on the moral high ground. In 1977, Canada under Trudeau's Liberals announced trade sanctions against apartheid South Africa and stated that it would withdraw support from any corporation doing business there. The U.S. didn't get around to sanctions until 1986, and even then Ronald Reagan tried to veto the bill in Congress. Americans make a big deal out of Nixon going to China in 1972, but China marked its first enjoyment of normal diplomatic relations in more than 20 years in North America with Canada first—a full year before Nixon went over.

Here are a few amazing individuals and episodes that caused our stock in the world to shoot up. A lot. And often when our neighbour was taking a difficult and sometimes even an opposite political stance.

Lester Pearson: Give Peace a Chance

Poor Mike; what he had to put up with. Yeah, they called him Mike, because "Lester" reinforced the image of the guy as an Elmer Fudd–like, hapless figure—and he was nothing of the sort. He was a talented athlete in his youth, a respected diplomat and a genuine patriot (he's the guy who saw to it that we finally had our own flag). It could be argued that until Trudeau, Lester Pearson did more to shape the current reputation of Canada than any other prime minister. He also knew how to stand up to Yanks. Long before he disagreed with LBJ over Vietnam, he had to tangle with America's most sinister law enforcement type and closet transvestite, J. Edgar Hoover. Guess what? He won.

When elected as prime minister in 1963, Pearson had already been annoying rabid right-wingers in America for a while. In 1951, when he was External Affairs Minister under Louis St. Laurent, he gave a speech to the Empire and Canadian clubs in Toronto, warning that the "easy" days of automatic relations were over, and Canada wasn't "willing to be merely an echo." When Americans sent him hate mail and Washington voiced its disapproval, he suggested it "confirms my thesis that we never get much attention down there unless we say something critical, and then the attention becomes surprised, pained and irritated."

This was the heyday of the McCarthy hearings, and anti-Communist paranoia had already infected the RCMP. One of Pearson's old friends, Herbert Norman—a skilled diplomat educated at Harvard and Cambridge—was running the U.S. desk at External Affairs and came under suspicion for his past association with leftist groups. The McCarthyites were crying Commie and spy. The Mounties investigated Norman but cleared him, and Pearson was one of his staunchest defenders. Back in

1949, Pearson saw the poison McCarthy was spreading across America and stated, "I hope we may never succumb to the black madness of the witch hunt."

Down in Washington, J. Edgar Hoover fumed. Keep in mind this is a guy who would later drag out the skeletons on the Kennedys to keep them in check. "Pearson had better stop mouthing his half-truths as pertain to the FBI," he grumbled. Of course, the G-men had a file on Pearson; it was 243 pages long under a heading of "Espionage R" (the "R" was for Russian). Hoover threatened to release the file for public scrutiny.

Pearson's answer? Go ahead. And Hoover backed down.

But that's not the end of the story—far from it. In 1956, when Egypt's leader, Gamal Nasser, seized control of the Suez Canal, which had always been run by foreign powers like Britain and France, it triggered an international crisis. Israel invaded Egypt while British and French bombers made the country's airfields into craters. Our man at the UN, Pearson suggested British and French forces withdraw while a new international peacekeeping force was sent in to bring stability back to the borders. It was the first time the UN ever sent peacekeepers, and such operations would become a staple of the organization's efforts at peace.

It was a Canadian who came up with it.

Off in Egypt, it was another Canadian, Herbert Norman, who at the height of the crisis was trying to negotiate with Nasser. Joe McCarthy was by then gone, the witch-hunt Senate hearings long over, but the Americans amazingly dragged out their tired old accusations about Herbert Norman being a Commie. Pearson again defended him in the House of Commons, but Norman had reached his breaking point. He jumped off the roof of a building in downtown Cairo and plunged eight stories to his death.

An MP for the Co-operative Commonwealth Foundation (the CCF, which became the NDP) called it "murder by slander." The *Toronto Star* seemed to agree, running as a headline, "Murder—MP." Helping to muddy the waters and fuel the conspiracy theories was the emergence of two suicide notes, which was a little strange. And outraged Canadians definitely felt less close to their American cousins for a while.

Joe McCarthy—who was destroyed by Edward R. Murrow on CBS and again when the U.S. Army pointed out that he tried to get one of his own flunkies out of the service—died of alcoholism the same year Norman died. Today J. Edgar Hoover is remembered as a vindictive, petty, closet bisexual cross-dresser whose name is synonymous with paranoia.

As for Pearson, a politician who stood by his friend and never buckled when faced with sleazy tactics, he got the Nobel Peace Prize for his work on the Suez Crisis, went on to become prime minister and got an airport named after him in Toronto.

Ken Taylor and the Canadian Caper

If you haven't heard the story of how Ken Taylor and other Canadians rescued Americans in Iran, shame on you—and if you have, chances are you never heard the entire bizarre story, which involved the CIA and a fake science fiction movie.

The incredible drama unfolded in November 1979 when student militants completely flouted one of the basic tenets of international law, scaled the walls of the U.S. embassy in Tehran and took over, capturing 70 hostages—all with the tacit support of Ayatollah

207

Khomenei. Over 444 days, the militants paraded out blindfolded and terrified hostages, and numerous stories have emerged of their humiliating treatment and sometimes torture during their captivity. Then Ronald Reagan's pals went behind the Carter administration's back to negotiate the hostages' release, but only *after* his swearing-in ceremony so he could look like a hero, all in trade for arms.

Six American diplomats had managed to slip away in the confusion of the demonstrations. When one American official on the run took the chance of calling John Sheardown, a friend at the Canadian embassy, Sheardown told him, "Why didn't you call sooner? Of course we can take you in."

Half the Americans hid at Sheardown's house and the other at Ken Taylor's official residence, both in the upscale district of Shemiran. As the weeks rolled on, the six Americans made the best of it and were quite comfortable with books, good food and even Scotch and beer. But the students knew some of their targets had escaped, and they were relentless in trying to get them back, even resorting to using professional carpet weavers to jigsaw back together shredded documents.

"We were perpetually worried," Ken Taylor told *Wired* magazine for an article on the caper in 2007. "We could have been caught, labelled persona non grata and asked to leave the country. We could have been thrown into the U.S. embassy. Or worse. It was dimmer prospects for the Americans had they been caught."

The Canadians were taking a huge risk in hiding the Americans. How could they get the Americans out of the country? Believe it or not, a high-ranking, clever CIA official, Tony Mendez, came up with an elaborate scheme to sneak the Americans out as—wait for it—film crew members scouting locations for a science fiction movie! The bogus film was to be based on Roger Zelazny's SF novel *Lord of Light,* which somebody actually did want to make into a movie and even had a script for it—until someone else embezzled production funds. Mendez knew Hollywood folk and enlisted the help of a special effects man and the makeup wizard on the original *Planet of the Apes* to create a phoney production studio.

The whole outrageous scheme worked because while Iran's fundamentalist revolutionaries were shouting "Death to America," scaring all the other embassies and taking their society back to the Middle Ages for a few years, believe it or not, the new government was actually looking for international business investments.

Although it's against the law to counterfeit Canadian official documents, Parliament held a secret emergency session—its first since World War Two—to green-light the manufacture of fake passports. Before the Americans donned their makeup and pretended to be filmmakers, a Farsi-speaking staff member of the Canadian embassy dressed up in fatigues and played "interrogator," helping them rehearse for any contingencies if suspicion was aroused. Then early in the morning of January 28, 1980, after about three months of hiding, the Americans stood in line to board a Swissair jet at Mehrabad Airport...and were waved through. Hours later, they were free and safe in Europe.

The CIA's role wouldn't be revealed for years, and now that it finally has been, there's even been some interest from Hollywood. A fake studio created as a high-stakes attempt to get Americans out of a hostile country? It's a natural, baby! I see George Clooney attached (which is apparently true—Clooney has expressed interest in the project). We can only hope if the filmmakers ever do retell the story, they remember our role.

When the Americans made it back safely, the U.S. was genuinely grateful. Ken Taylor became an overnight hero and received the well-deserved Order of Canada. He had the more dubious honour of a permed Gordon Pinsent portraying him in a TV mini-series.

Robert Anders, one of the escaped Americans, probably offered the highest compliment in gratitude. He told *Wired* that for a course on terrorism, he was once asked what the lessons were from his experience. "I thought about it and said, 'Wherever you go in the world, if you're going to be there a while, be sure to make friends with the Canadians.'"

Joe Clark to the Rescue

Conservatives are supposed to be hawks, and yet in the age when Reagan was sending soldiers to Grenada and Thatcher dispatched troops to save sheep from the Argentines on the Falkland Islands, Brian Mulroney— their pal—had an external affairs minister in the 1980s who helped increase Canada's prestige by being a dove.

Joe Clark had held Mulroney's job himself a few years prior. But back then, inexperienced and awkward, he had tried to run a minority government as if he had a majority. Our political cartoonists had a field day with him (one of them depicted poor "Joe Who?" under the shadow of Skylab, then in its decaying orbit). Clark was soon out of office on a no-confidence motion.

As External Affairs Minister, however, Clark began to sound like the conscience of the world, and the world listened. He led the call for economic sanctions to punish the apartheid regime in South Africa when Reagan and Thatcher didn't want them. Clark didn't like how the Americans were mucking about in Nicaragua, backing the Contra rebels despite the 1984 elections being considered free and fair by international observers (including ours). He told them so. That same year, the famine in Ethiopia caught worldwide attention, and Clark became the very first foreign affairs minister from a developed nation to visit.

"I thought someone else was going to do something, the United States or the United Kingdom," Mulroney recalled later for the CBC. "I didn't know. I was brand new. And when, after a couple of days or so, nothing had happened, Joe Clark and I got together. I said, 'Joe, I know you share my view. We've got to do something about this immediately. No one else appears to be doing anything'."

Ethiopia at the time was still ruled by the brutal Derg, the military junta that had murdered the country's emperor, Haile Selassie, but Canada broke ranks with Western powers shunning the Marxist regime. Clark, who hadn't yet even seen footage of the famine, rerouted a return flight from India to Ethiopia, arriving ahead of UN leaders with our new emergency coordinator, David MacDonald. He promised help was coming, and it was. Canada immediately offered $50 million, with donations coming in from ordinary citizens across the country. The CBC later estimated, "Before the end, Canada alone saved perhaps 700,000 of more than seven million lives spared by emergency relief."

Norman Bethune: 1.3 Billion Chinese Can't Be Wrong

Academics and some politicians in the U.S. still occasionally talk about how America "lost" China—when the truth is no one ever had it, except for the Japanese, who could only take pieces of it. This myth was largely constructed out of the experiences of a bad-tempered American general, Joseph Stilwell, known as "Vinegar Joe," who from 1935 until 1939 served as military attaché to the U.S. legation in Beijing and who later, during World War Two, was made commander of the China-Burma-India Theatre, as well as chief of staff to Generalissimo Chiang Kai-shek, who headed the Nationalist forces.

Stilwell argued with Chiang about how to fight the Japanese. He argued with a lot of people, including his fellow Allied commanders. To be fair, Stilwell was fluent in Chinese and had respect for the Chinese people. He didn't have respect for Chiang Kai-shek, whom he took to calling "the little dummy" and "Peanut." The Nationalists under Chiang were disgustingly corrupt, while their conscripted troops were ineffectual, hopelessly starved and always on the brink of desertion.

It's one thing to have an incompetent dictator as your ally; it's another thing to suggest to that same ally that an American should take charge of his army. That's exactly what Franklin Roosevelt did in 1944, telling Chiang he knew of "no other man who has the ability, force and the determination to offset the disaster that now threatens China." Obviously, FDR's War Department didn't consider Mao Zedong. He clearly didn't think of any other Chinese person either—even though another American general later described the Communist fighters as "better men physically... better fed, better clothed...with better morale than the Nationalist troops."

In the end, Chiang Kai-shek lobbied Washington to pull Stilwell out of China. Once Japan was defeated, the alliance between the Nationalists and the Communists broke down, and the two sides resumed a bloody civil war until Mao's Communist army pushed Chiang's forces all the way to what is now Taiwan. "Stilwell's mission was America's supreme try in China," historian Barbara Tuchman wrote in her biography of the general. The line has a nice missionary ring to it, doesn't it? Tuchman ended her book more wisely with, "In the end China went her own way as if the Americans had never come."

In contrast to an American general trying to prop up a dictator he despised, a Canadian communist went over to China before the outbreak of World War Two to heal ordinary soldiers and civilians. And his legend is still told to Chinese children in storybooks, his name still a household word: Norman Bethune.

The son of a Presbyterian minister in Gravenhurst, Ontario, Bethune was a larger-than-life eccentric personality, a brilliant surgeon and a gifted amateur artist. When he contracted tuberculosis in the 1920s, he kept smoking and arranged parties at his sanatorium in upstate New York, smuggling wine in from Québec. Depressed, he painted a 60-foot mural along the walls of his cottage on the hospital grounds, which depicted him carried into and out of the world by angels, with symbolic galleons, castles and wild beasts in between. He regularly performed pneumothorax (compression therapy) on himself for his TB, which involved artificially collapsing his own lung. After his recovery, he went to teach in Montréal, where he developed new techniques in thoracic surgery and designed new surgical instruments, one of which is still in use today.

But Bethune also began to pay attention to the economics of being sick. When he went to Memphis, Tennessee, to present a paper on anaesthesia, he delivered a passionate call for socialized medicine (oh, oh, there it is again). The Memphis newspapers made sure they ignored this part of his speech. Growing more radicalized, Bethune went off to fight the fascists in Spain and developed the world's first mobile medical unit.

His work in China built his true legacy. By then he was a firm communist, and, working early morning to late at night behind the front lines, he was always at a loss for basic supplies and equipment as he trained doctors, organized medical services and performed surgery right on the battlefield. None of that mattered. "It is true that I am tired, but I don't think I have been so happy for a long time," he wrote. "I am content. I am doing what I want to do." One of the supplies regularly missing was rubber gloves, and he contracted fatal blood poisoning from a cut he received during surgery in late November 1939. The Chinese couldn't find a Canadian emblem, so they draped his coffin with an American flag.

Mao Zedong wrote an essay that would soon become required reading in China's schools, praising Bethune for "his utter devotion to others" and admitting that Zedong himself was "deeply grieved over his death." Bethune became, for a long time, the most recognized hero of the revolution after Mao himself.

It's astonishing how Bethune's memory is kept alive and well in China even today. There have been commemorative stamps. Jilin University has the Norman Bethune College of Medicine, with its own museum for him. At Shijiazhuang, Hebei Province, stands a hospital in his honour, and his statue stands in a memorial park nearby. In the same city, at the Revolutionary Martyrs' Cemetery where he's buried, a large memorial hall bears his name, and every year on the anniversary of his death special ceremonies are held at his tomb. There's yet another Bethune Memorial Hall in the Wutai Mountain region.

He has had at least two biopics of his life made in China, one produced in 1964 (in this one, he's depicted as a bland but kindly, almost Santa Clause–like hero figure) and a more recent one in 2006. The second one was a lavish 20-part miniseries for China Central Television, the most expensive Chinese series ever made, with a budget of 30 million yuan ($4.7 million).

The film's young female director, Yang Yang, called the subject of the series "an interesting man, a good doctor and a good friend. I wanted to depict him as a person and not as some kind of remote hero."

She must have done a good job in portraying Bethune's gradual change from privileged, flamboyant physician to healer of the people. One fan admitted to the *People's Daily Online* that in the final episode, when peasants line up in the snow as Bethune's body is carried out, he cried. "It reminds us that there is something in this world more important than money." (Okay, sure, it's the *People's Daily*, which is propaganda, but who knows? Maybe the guy really was moved.)

An international reputation grows and evolves on more than what governments do. It also develops from how our citizens behave abroad and what they do. More than a billion Chinese people know about the selfless dedication of one Canadian. Not too shabby.

THIRTEEN
Education

THE DOG ATE MY
RESEARCH FOR THIS SECTION

LET'S IGNORE THE OTHER GROANERS about getting an "A" or "high marks" and just say we do remarkably well when it comes to education. As far as the stats go...now because I didn't go to university and can't understand the confusing charts and tables on the OECD's most up-to-date report of international comparisons in education, I cribbed some of the following from a story in 2009 by Peter O'Neil, who has been a Canwest News Europe correspondent (hey, at least I didn't crib them from Wikipedia entries or beg for them on Craigslist, like certain college students do).

It turns out Canada has the highest percentage of 25- to 34-year-olds who have moved on to get a university or community college education, about 55 percent. More than the U.S., and more than the rest of the OECD nations. We seem to have a high population of nerds, too—Canada ranks sixth out of 28 countries when the science skills of 15-year-olds are assessed. Don't worry, Canadian geeks, being sexually active is just around the corner...of your master's. But hey, later you'll earn more, and it'll be worth it.

When it comes to a percentage of our gross domestic product devoted to education, we rank sixth out of the 34 OECD countries, at 6.5 percent. "The high price tag for education is blamed on post-secondary education costs, pegged at 2.7 percent of GDP," O'Neil reported in 2009. "That is second only to the U.S. figure of 2.9 percent, and almost double the OECD average of 1.4 percent." In dollars, our students aren't shelling out as much as Americans do to get a diploma, but

217

they still pay plenty. In 2005, for instance, a Canadian student paid an average of $25,266 US dollars while his American counterpart spent more than $56,000.

That doesn't necessarily mean our students are getting a bargain. A research group, the Educational Policy Institute, put out a report in 2006 that suggested poorer states in the U.S. tend to be more affordable "both because tuition is usually low compared to other states and because federal student aid acts as an equalizing force. In Canada, poorer provinces tend to be less affordable both because tuition is higher than in other provinces and because the tendency of wealthier provinces to spend more heavily on student aid counteracts the equalizing effects of federal student aid programs."

The U.S. still shows wide discrepancies between how people of different ethnic backgrounds excel in university, with only 25 percent of African-Americans achieving a bachelor's degree, according to the U.S. Census Bureau's figures in 2003. The OECD noted in 2006 how Canada, unlike the U.S., was "among countries in which social background has the smallest impact on student success," but at the same time about a third of Canadian families have admitted that financial difficulties prevent a son or daughter from going on to get a higher education. Rather than your race or where you're from in Canada, it's whether or not you have the bucks that decides if you get to put fancy letters on your resume.

COMPARISONS FOR
(OF) DUMMIES

NEVER LET US FORGET, HOWEVER, that there's a big difference between knowledge and education. In 2009, the Intercollegiate Studies Institute discovered that most Americans from all backgrounds couldn't answer simple questions about history, basic economics and civics. Only half could name all three branches of the U.S. government, and one in five thought the Electoral College either "trains those aspiring for higher office" or "was established to supervise the first televised presidential debates." It's interesting how cultural and economic bias crept into the phrasing of the questions, which included number 27, "Free markets typically secure more economic prosperity than government's centralized planning because..."

Free markets "typically secure" more prosperity all by themselves, eh? He who wrote this line must stay after class and read the Business (see page 36), History (see page 91) and Environment and Natural Resources (see page 67) sections of this book—there will be a quiz later. And, oh yeah, go study some grammar because your syntax is awful. We could go into why you shouldn't use "typically" in this sentence, but we're busy bashing your people over civics at the moment.

But let's not get smug. Canadians are horribly ignorant when it comes to our history as well, as discovered in a study by Ipsos Reid and the Dominion Institute. The 2007 study found that less than half of the Canadians it quizzed who were aged 18 to 24 could name our first prime minister and only one-quarter could offer the right date for Confederation. And despite the pathetic low scores, only 5 percent of participants thought the questions were too difficult! In other words, they knew they were embarrassingly ignorant. The one shining ray of encouragement is that at least their knowledge of our military history had improved a little over a previous study's findings.

J.L. Granatstein, who wrote the groundbreaking *Who Killed Canadian History?*, would most likely not be surprised by the findings. In his bestselling book, Granatstein pointed out that Canadian students get to learn how our historical landscape is marked with racist, sexist milestones—such as how Canada's first doctor, Emily Stowe, had to deal with a patriarchal medical establishment and how Japanese Canadians were mistreated in World War Two—but very little about our Fathers of Confederation or Frederick Banting or how well we did at Normandy on D-Day (or how our Canadians defending Hong Kong wound up in atrocity-ridden Japanese prisoner-of-war camps). No wonder young people remain ignorant about who we are.

Just as both Canadians and Americans have to look up dates in the encyclopedia, we also both reach for our calculators. In 2008, a study by the American Mathematical Society (yep, there really is one) found the U.S. isn't doing enough to develop the math skills of both boys and girls. Meanwhile up in Canada, an academic at BC's Simon Fraser University, Arvind Gupta has bemoaned our poor numeracy skills. "Our system is very child focused," he told the *Toronto Star* in a short profile piece in 2009. "We tell kids, 'Do what you find fun. If math is hard for you, then try something else.'"

Gupta pointed out that studies have shown children begin loving math—at least 85 percent of kids do—in grade three. But by grade eight, that figure plummets to 25 percent. And ignorance breeds ignorance. "Their parents are starting to struggle at that level," said Gupta. "The teachers aren't really well versed beyond that level. And so the kids fall off."

On both sides of the border, the experts agree that if anyone is carrying the math torch, it's the children of immigrants. Foreign students, for instance, make up half of those doing graduate studies in maths and sciences. American and Canadian graduate degree rankings for these subjects, when compared to the rest of the world, are abysmal—in the U.S., it's 0.7 percent while in Canada it's 0.4 percent. But for us, the news gets worse. As the *Star* reported, "Studies suggest that, owing to lack of opportunity here, half of [graduates in these subjects] will be working outside of Canada within two years of graduation."

Yanks and Canucks are both slowpokes in the marathon, but our team may also be leaving the track.

FOURTEEN
Science and Technology

IF YOU WATCH LONG
ENOUGH, YOU MIGHT SEE THE
BUDGET EVOLVING

As with education, we have to say our full lab results for Canada versus the U.S. aren't in yet.

Right from his inaugural address, President Barack Obama promised to "restore science to its rightful place, and wield technology's wonders to raise health care's quality and lower its cost." By late June 2009, the House of Representatives passed a bill allocating $30.6 billion for investments in science, technology and innovation, with $6.9 billion going to the National Science Foundation.

While the congressional bill escaped being a casualty of cuts related to the recession, the funding for science in the Harper government's latest budget was reaching critical mass—that is to say, a mass of criticism. Harper, whose previous budgets got failing grades from scientists, insisted in late January 2009 that his government would commit another $5 billion to science, a good chunk of it to improve lab facilities at colleges and universities. Those in the white coats replied there's not much point beefing up lab infrastructure when Ottawa was cutting $148 million over three years from the agencies that fund the research carried out in those labs.

Martin Godbout, the head of Genome Canada— the non-profit agency that funds major science and genetics projects—publicly expressed his astonishment that his organization was left out of the budget

223

CANADA VS. THE UNITED STATES

altogether, whereas it had received $140 million in the 2008 budget and $100 million in 2007. "It's like we fell between the chairs," he told the CBC. "This was an infrastructure budget, and so money went into that, but we got nothing."

Harper's Minister for Science and Technology, Gary Goodyear, defended his government's position by saying Genome Canada was still getting funds from previous budgets. That was cold comfort to Godbout, who was worried about money for new initiatives.

Commercializing research has been the focus of the government's policy. When he spoke to the *Globe and Mail*, Goodyear's vision of science and technology in Canada had as many pricing guns as it did cyclotrons. "If we are going to be serious about saving lives and improving life around this planet, if we are serious about helping the environment, then we are going to have to get some of these technologies out of the labs onto the factory floors. Made. Produced. Sold. And that is going to fulfill that talk. So yes, we have to do all of it, we have to do discovery...but it can't end there."

Critics pointed out that even a recession-hit U.S. found the money to support both infrastructure and cutting-edge research.

Goodyear, of course, has never been a hit with the geek crowd. Although he took undergraduate courses in physics and chemistry at the University of Waterloo, his former career before government was as a chiropractor. In exploring rumours that Harper's man for science was a creationist, the *Globe and Mail* asked him pointedly whether he believed in evolution. Goodyear refused to answer the question.

Oh, boy. The lab coats really didn't like that.

When CTV's *Power Play* cornered him on the issue, he admitted he did believe in evolution—then suggested the idea of a conflict between holding his portfolio and being a creationist was "absolutely ridiculous" and had "no relevance."

For Canada's scientists, it couldn't be more relevant. One biology professor at Queen's University in Kingston argued that a science minister should be able to weigh science "just as the finance minister should be able to assess information from financial people."

A biologist at Newfoundland's Memorial University, Steven Carr told the CBC, "If the minister were asked if he accepts the theory of global warming—an evolutionary phenomenon that will have massive impact on plant and animal species in the coming decades—I hope he would not say that environmental change is irrelevant to his portfolio."

The question hardly needs to be put to Obama's so-called science czar, the director of the U.S. Office of Science and Technology Policy, John Holdren. He went to MIT and has a PhD from Stanford, places where he learned aeronautics and plasma physics. He taught at Harvard for 13 years and for more than two decades at Berkley. He was also one of Bill Clinton's science advisors, and his work has focused on global environmental change and energy technology.

Hmmm.... One way to measure someone's priorities is to see who they put in charge.

Politics aside (and when the money's available), Canada can certainly hold its own in science and technology, especially when it comes to medical and pharmaceutical research—this is, after all, the land of Banting, Bethune and Osler. It was a Nova Scotian, Dr. Kevin Ogilvie, who discovered how to synthesize RNA and who helped invent the first automated gene synthesizer. A team of Canadians led by Dr. Philip Seeman identified dopamine receptors as factors in schizophrenia, and for their labours they got France's prestigious Prix Galien in 1994.

A Small Sample of Canadian Inventions and Scientific Discoveries

What Inventions	Who	When
pacemaker	Dr. John Alexander Hopps	first prototype 1950; first successful implant 1958
Ski-Doo	Armand Bombardier	first prototype 1922, first patent 1937
Pablum	Dr. Theodore Drake, Dr. Alan Brown	1930
Trivial Pursuit	Scott Abbott, Chris Haney	1979; became available internationally in 1982
"separable fastener" a.k.a. zipper	Gideon Sundback	patented in 1913
basketball	James Naismith	1891
Robertson screw	Peter Lymburner Robertson	patented 1909
Discoveries	Who	When
insulin	Frederick Banting, Dr. John Macleod	1922; won Nobel Prize in 1923 for the discovery
catalytic RNA	Sid Altman	won Nobel Prize in 1989 for the discovery
how to extract helium from natural gas	John Cunningham McLennan	1915

We also have Willard Boyle, who was one of the co-creators of the first continuously operating ruby laser. In addition, he was awarded the Nobel Prize in

Physics in 2009 for his work with a colleague, George Smith, 40 years earlier on the charge-coupled device (CCD). (The CCD is an integral component in the majority of today's digital cameras, turning light into electrical signals.) It should be noted that Boyle and Smith's award, however, has become controversial, because their former colleagues at Bell Labs down in New Jersey say they don't deserve it.

The man that some say should have gotten the prize, Mike Tompsett, has insisted, "Willard Boyle was a high-level manager and didn't do anything at all as far as the development's concerned. And George Smith had moved off CCDs within about three or four months, and he played no active part in it either. I was the one who did all the work...They got the patent for inventing the concept. They really did not anticipate imaging."

But he grumbles that there's nothing that can be done about it. Interestingly, the rival parties involved in the controversy never liked working together, so again, hmmmm....

Those who contest Boyle's award say it's not a vendetta. Boyle has another name for it: sour grapes.

We may never know, and the Nobel committee doesn't have to care—under the rules, once the award's given, it can't be revoked.

CANADA IN SPACE

Look, the Canadarm Is Waving!

The pride we Canadians take in our contributions to space resembles a classic episode of *The Simpsons*.

In "Deep Space Homer," the sitcom's hero, Homer Simpson, becomes an astronaut. He's NASA's "Joe Six-Pack" choice to help save its dwindling support among the American public (the episode is so popular with NASA, a DVD copy was sent on a supply ship to the International Space Station). In the climax, Homer breaks an inanimate carbon rod off the wall of the space shuttle to defend himself in a goofy struggle with another astronaut. As a result, he winds up accidentally sealing the shuttle's broken door, saving himself and the crew. But instead of Homer being praised as a hero, the carbon rod is given its own ticker-tape parade and gets on magazine covers like *Time* with the headline "In Rod We Trust."

Canada's space pride is like that. While American astronauts got all the glory, we kept cheering the Canadarm. Way to go, inanimate metal arm! You rock.

Fortunately, now we can also cheer our astronauts like Marc Garneau, Roberta Bondar, Steve MacLean, Julie Payette and Chris Hadfield. And as it turns out with so many things, America didn't go into the heavens alone—it had Canadian help practically from the beginning.

Canadarm: Some Reach, Eh?

It started with a sales call in the 1970s. Canadian engineer Lloyd Secord was originally trying to sell a space telescope. Not interested, said NASA. But wait! There's more! Secord was working on a robot arm. Hmmmm, said NASA, we could use one of those.... It took years, with Spar Aerospace as the lead contractor and more than $100 million from the Canadian government to develop, but in February 1981, NASA got its first Canadarm.

It has deployed satellites, and it has retrieved satellites. It has moved a Plasma Diagnostics Package and a science platform. It has even done plumbing in space, removing clogged wastewater on a space shuttle. ("New Toilet Duck, now with Canadian space technology!") When the Hubble Space Telescope was becoming an international joke because it just plain didn't work, the Canadarm was key to its repair and upgrade in 1993. And it's still being used in space missions today, almost 30 years after its development. Americans talk about one big step, but what they always need is a good Canadian grasp.

Several Small Steps for Canadians...

Jim Chamberlin had once been an engineer for Canada's ill-fated Avro Arrow project (which, as it turns out, was a failure we can't blame on the Americans, as much as some of us would like to). After Avro was scrapped, he got one of the top jobs at NASA's Mercury program and was considered "the brains behind Gemini." It was Chamberlin, a Canadian, who came up with the idea of the lunar module. Another Canadian, Owen Maynard, rose to become chief of systems engineering and then chief of mission operations for Apollo.

We knew Canada had really arrived in space, however, when Marc Garneau became our first astronaut. NASA had invited us to send up our people as far back as the late seventies. As Chris Gainor writes in *Canada in Space*, a number of developments were behind the invitation. "The first space traveller who was neither American nor Soviet was Vladimir Remek of Czechoslovakia [in 1978]. The propaganda impact of these flights was not lost on NASA." Hmmm, might be good to send up a Canuck.

The Americans kept inviting us in 1978 and 1981, until finally we got our act together in 1983, and Ottawa officially launched the Canadian Astronaut Program...by placing a want ad. Hey, it worked for our spies, didn't it? (See page 240).

Most of the 4380 people who responded were unsuitable, but a five-member panel of the National Research Council did manage to find Marc Garneau. As a payload specialist aboard the *Challenger* space shuttle, Garneau went about his business with the discipline he'd learned as a Canadian Forces naval officer, making sure he didn't chatter to the ground crew and interfere with his American colleagues' work. A Canadian reporter, failing to appreciate Garneau had a job to do up there, peevishly dubbed him "the Right Stiff" for not providing enough quotable comments. But our first man in space proved himself to American astronauts. His shuttle commander, Bob Crippen, said, "I would be pleased to fly with Marc or any other Canadian astronaut."

Garneau paved the way for Roberta Bondar, Steve MacLean, Robert Thirsk and others. Chris Hadfield and Julie Payette helped build the International Space Station.

Garneau, who was president of the Canadian Space Agency for five years before he went into politics, has pushed for Canadians to be more than technology providers and occasional astronauts for NASA. In 2002, he proposed a Canadian-built spacecraft to explore Mars, one that "would feature Canadian ideas, technologies and expertise."

We've yet to see Canadian-built spacecraft reaching the Red Planet, but we have gone to Mars and proved our unique ideas and expertise. It was a Canadian-built, $37-million meteorological station aboard the Phoenix Mars Lander that found snow and ice-water clouds on the Red Planet in 2008.

INTERNET:
PAGE CANNOT BE DISPLAYED

THIS BOOK WILL NOT BE downloadable from the publisher's website. Not only would we not make money if we did that, but knowing how Internet service is in this country, we might hear mouses thrown against walls and screams through gritted teeth from Prince George to Moncton. In October 2009, a Harvard study told us what too many of us already knew: compared to the U.S. and the rest of the developed world, Canada has some of the poorest high-speed Internet service, and it's so God-awful embarrassing, it's an example of what *not* to do.

The doorstop of a report was made by Harvard's Berkman Center for Internet and Society. Its purpose was to help the U.S. Federal Communications Commission figure out a national next-generation broadband plan for Americans. And it concluded that we're way down the list when it comes to a peer country comparison over things like network capacity and prices. We ranked 22nd overall out of 30 countries; 16th on broadband adoption, 20th on speed and capacity, and possibly most galling of all, 25th when it comes to affordability. Japan, Sweden and South Korea headed the list, with the U.S. at the 13th spot.

The Harvard researchers concluded that if America wants to be a leader when it comes to broadband, it should look to the open-access policies used in Europe and Asia to increase competition among service providers. They say flatly that the American and Canadian approach, which relies on competition between cable and phone companies to develop better and cheaper services, is definitely not the way to go.

"Early aggressive facilities-based competition certainly made Canada an early starter, but it does not seem to have enabled it to maintain its standing," said the report. "The Canadian experience suggest[s] that reliance purely on competition between strong cable incumbents and telephony incumbents may be insufficient to sustain high penetration or achieve high capacity and low competitive pricing in the long term."

The report also criticized Canada for a "half-hearted" approach to open access, which allows a new player in the market to lease lines from a network owner to provide its own Internet services to customers. The CRTC brought in open-access rules in 1997, but the researchers argue that the commission messed them up. How did they do that? Apparently, by letting network owners charge the highest lease rates in the developed world—they're about 70 percent higher than similar fees in South Korea and Denmark.

Such high rates and "regulatory hesitance," said the report, probably contributed to fewer new competitors making investments. And it didn't like the CRTC's recent "self-congratulatory reference" to Canada's leadership of G7 nations in terms of broadband adoption. Adoption is just one yardstick, according to the researchers, and they found "almost all of the Canadian companies in the cluster with the slowest speeds and highest prices."

The president of the University of Waterloo, David Johnston, pointed out that Harvard isn't the only source of a damning report on our broadband.

"The reality is our rates are considerably higher than most leading countries...The measurement of Canada's standing in world broadband and that declining trajectory is pretty clear from numerous studies. I really don't think there's much dispute that we don't occupy the same spot as we did 15 years ago."

We're looking at *you*, Bell, Rogers and Telus (or as we customers prefer to call you, the Forces of Darkness).

And what does Ottawa think of all this? Well, as life went on and the Harvard study was pushed aside for other news, it looks like it's just business as usual for our regulators and the big firms behind broadband. While the federal government overturned the commission in December 2009 and let in a new wireless service provider, Globalive, (which is backed by Egypt's Orascom), it made other decisions that suggest not much will change for us...you know, the actual customers that these companies are supposed to serve.

For instance, the government reversed an order that would have forced the big companies to offer the same speed services they sell to smaller regional ISPs, like Teksavvy or Execulink, at reasonable rates.

The smaller ISPs rent portions of the big boys' networks to offer their own services. But they've been stuck selling Internet speeds up to around five megabits per second, while Bell and Telus can provide up to 15 or 16 megabits. Bell and Telus appealed the CRTC's decision, and as this modest tome is being drafted, the government has told the commission to review its decision and get back to it by the autumn of 2010. Don't hold out too much hope for the Davids to defeat the ISP Goliaths.

Meanwhile, also in December 2009, the U.S. Federal Communications Commission called for a re-allocation of funds for America's rural and low-income citizens, who weren't getting decent broadband.

FIFTEEN
Cool Spy Stuff

THE NAME IS PINE...
JACK PINE

SSHHHHH! DON'T TELL ANYONE, but we're better at this stuff than you might think. Mind you, we didn't necessarily start out that way, and the U.S. has been there all along, sometimes helping, sometimes screwing things up, sometimes our ally, sometimes wearing a dark trench coat, so to speak, and talking into its lapel. And sometimes outright encouraging evil right within our borders.

THE MENGELE IN
MONTRÉAL

A DARK CHAPTER FOR BOTH OUR international relations and the history of espionage in Canada happened when the CIA employed a Scottish-American sociopath with a medical degree, one Dr. Donald Ewen Cameron, to conduct mind control experiments on his patients at the Allan Memorial Institute in Montréal in the 1960s. Patients who came to Cameron with minor complaints like anxiety disorders or post-partum depression were often doped with LSD and other drugs without their consent and subjected to bizarre experiments, such as having to endure tape loops of noise. Many suffered mental traumas that lasted for years afterward, and when they tried to sue and go public with their stories, their fellow Canadians often didn't believe them.

Lest you think this story is too fantastic and has been made up, it's been well documented in several court cases, described in several books, written up in articles in the *Washington Post* and *New York Times* and made into a couple of disappointing TV movies. One of Cameron's victims was the wife of prominent Manitoba MP David Orlikow. Velma Orlikow was one of eight brave victims who stepped forward to sue the CIA—and won, getting an out-of-court settlement.

The Canadian government wasn't much help to the victims—not surprising when you learn that back in the 1950s, Health and Welfare Canada gave the Institute one-half million dollars in funding for the experiments. Decades later, when victims stepped forward to sue, the Mulroney government, clearly fearing Ottawa's own liability, suppressed key evidence (CIA officials had apparently apologized to the Canadian government, admissions of wrongdoing that could have been used in court).

And what became of Cameron's "findings" from his creepy experiments in Montréal? They were developed into interrogation, sleep deprivation and torture techniques that the CIA put into a now infamous manual and taught to right-wing regimes in Latin America, Iran under the Shah and parts of the Middle East that are still using them today.

Sad to say, but the roots of Abu Ghraib and various nightmares of international espionage can be traced right back to Montréal, where the Company was fooling around with brainwashing.

WHO WATCHES
THE WATCHERS?

ESPIONAGE AND COUNTER-INTELLIGENCE used to be handled mostly by the Mounties through its Security Service. Its officers even had their own dress uniform in brown instead of red serge—not that they wore them much. They were forbidden to wear them for weddings or on their way to formal functions, so that *not* wearing a uniform, dress or standard, became a tip-off that a Mountie had joined the Security Service.

When it came down to it, the Mounties were never truly suited to or comfortable with playing spy. They were cops—their job was to catch criminals and put them away, not "turn" them or monitor them or hatch elaborate ops to win the Cold War. So in 1977, when it emerged they were doing illegal and downright goofy stuff like break-ins and a barn burning (really) to pursue Québec separatists, their image suffered. As investigative journalist John Sawatsky put it in his book, *Men in the Shadows*, "The Mounties posing for tourists on Parliament Hill occasionally were asked for more familiar poses such as a furtive crouch behind a window."

But under the Mounties, we did come up with a crack surveillance unit that was unlike anything anywhere else, even in the States: they were called the Watcher Service. Watchers were so good even other Security Service staff couldn't tell they were being tailed. "They followed us around the city of Ottawa for three hours, and I never saw one Watcher's car," recalled one officer. "Not once. I looked around. I did everything to try and identify them. Not one car." Even the FBI was impressed, and it was ready to adopt their methods until J. Edgar Hoover squashed the idea—it offended his ego that his G-men could learn anything from Canadians.

The FBI, of course, was always chummy with the Mounties. The Feds' liaison officer for 15 years, Moss Innes was so cosy with them he often forgot himself while at the RCMP HQ and gave orders to our officers.

After everyone learned the Mounties could commit crimes in the name of national security as much as police them, it was decided we should have a separate spy agency. And recruitment for the Canadian Security Intelligence Service (CSIS) was done in very Canadian way. Through PriceWaterhouseCoopers, CSIS put out large want ads in newspapers such as the *Globe and Mail*. I can confirm this because I applied, for my own amusement, despite having a severe eyesight problem at the time—and kept my rejection letter proudly displayed on my bathroom wall for two years. (Twenty years later, Britain's MI5 turned over a new leaf in openness and also put recruitment ads in newspapers).

CSIS had very public growing pains. It particularly came under fire when it failed to prevent the 1985 Air India bombing, which had an investigation that remains controversial to this day. Some critics suggested the fledgling security service still had its head stuck in the Cold War shadows, chasing Russians while far worse terrorist threats to Canada were emerging out of ethnic and religious conflicts that its mostly white, unilingual officers had no clue about. Some blamed its spymasters for being too much in ideological sympathy with their counterparts down south.

It's a criticism that may still have truth in it. J. Michael Cole worked for CSIS for about three years and then quit to work for the *Taipei Times* in Taiwan. You would think his insightful 2008 book, *Smokescreen: Canadian*

Security Intelligence after September 11, 2001, would have caused more of a stir in our media.

Especially when it was highly critical of the service. Especially when it knocked CSIS for being so tight with U.S. intelligence interests.

But there was not a peep. The book made no noise on the CBC or the other networks. In addition, Cole says, Canada's biggest publishers balked at the chance to print his analysis. "As this was the first book on the subject to be published in many years, I think most of them were afraid of taking it. Canada's Security of Information laws are, ironically, more stringent than those in the US and are more like in the UK...."

What does Cole think of how CSIS does its job these days and its relationship with American intelligence? He says there's a lack of strategic thinking at CSIS that leaves it unable to determine what's in the interest of Canadians and what isn't. "The top management seems to care more about playing with the 'big boys'—the CIA, the FBI, MI5, MI6, the Israelis—than about ensuring that Canadians feel safe when they go to bed at night."

Cole argues that a lack of strategic guidance from above has meant CSIS often operates as if it were in a vacuum, a problem compounded by many intelligence officers, new and seasoned, who can't be bothered to read about current events, let alone history. "They focus on their targets at the exclusion of everything else and fail to place their actions in a larger context. When you remove that context, you also dehumanize the subject as the 'other.' The enemy becomes uprooted, no longer the product of historical continuities and discontinuities. In other words, the targets become mere pixels in a video game."

He says CSIS is still a "toddler in the game of intelligence," one that's been forced to grow up after 9/11.

"It is bedazzled by all those incoming lights and noise, but unfortunately it doesn't have enough experience to comprehend the dangers...In fact, the adult figure is encouraging the child to run straight into the traffic and to hell with the consequences."

Guess who the adult is in this scenario.

Cole says that soon after 9/11, CSIS "began recruiting agents like there's no tomorrow" in a drive that continues to this day, despite our small population.

"To be honest, based on my exchanges with my counterparts down south, the same phenomenon, the same lack of intellectual power, is in the U.S. intelligence community," says Cole. "I remember a trace request by a U.S. agency that shall remain unnamed about a suspected group of Islamic terrorists using a white van to carry 'stuff.' One need not be the mother of all spies to realize the futility of proceeding with the ally's request when the suspected individuals are actually fruit vendors from Mexico. But then again, they're brown-skinned. And in this brave new world of ours, sadly, brown-skinned is often construed as 'the other,' as a source of danger. It's ignorance mixed with racism mixed with the absence of consequences for those who screw up."

THE CSE:
"WE THOUGHT IT WOULD BE A FUN THING TO DO"

CSIS FALLS UNDER AN ACT OF Parliament, but it turns out since the 1950s we've also had our own secret foreign signals intelligence service (just like the National Security Agency), what today is known as the Communications Security Establishment or CSE.

Until fairly recently, the CSE often ran as an "NSA North" with no parliamentary oversight and a big, honking satellite dish on its Ottawa building just for messages zipping back and forth to the NSA's headquarters in Maryland. Not coincidentally, many CSE staff trained at the NSA's Fort Meade centre. In the mid-1990s, it came out that the hundreds of CSE employees sitting with headphones in a building on Ottawa's Heron Road thought nothing of spying on our own allies, such as Japan. The CSE also listened in on Mexico for negotiations leading up to the 1992 NAFTA agreement.

CSE has had little compunction as well about listening in on Canadians. Back in 1975, it helped out the Mounties by spying on Prime Minister Trudeau's flaky wife, Margaret, to find out if she was buying marijuana (when you show up on the front page of newspapers partying with the Rolling Stones away from your husband, yeah, the buttoned-down boys in red serge might go snooping). In the 1990s, a former CSE linguist, Jane Shorten, was eventually sacked after she complained to her supervisor about the dubious value and unethical standards of listening in on fellow Canadians, including one woman talking to her doctor about gynaecological problems. "I was just appalled. I talked to the senior linguist and said, 'I can't believe this. It's outrageous. I shouldn't be listening to this.'"

Sometimes even Mother England has asked our guys to come eavesdrop for her. Mother England in this case, of course, being a paranoid battle-axe who later liked to crush unionized miners and keep South American dictators as house guests. In 1983, Margaret Thatcher was the UK's prime minister, and on her orders CSE staff members were put up at a swanky London hotel so they could spy on two of her own cabinet ministers.

In a tell-all memoir, ex-CSE agent Mike Frost described the incident. He wrote, "The moral issue wasn't raised. We listened so routinely to private conversations we were not supposed to hear that I guess we had become immune to that kind of soul-searching...In the end, we just thought it would be a fun thing to do."

Frost also pointed out that back when the U.S. embassy sat at 100 Wellington Street across from Parliament Hill, the building had rather suspicious looking "air vents" and "heat pumps," which he was certain were actually protected intercept antennae for spying on us. The Americans, he was shocked to discover, were doing to its ally what it taught Canada to do to other nations.

So should we put up with this? Why couldn't we simply "jam" them? It's a question even Frost's co-author, Michel Gratton, asked.

The answer seems to be it would be bad spy etiquette.

"Deliberate and effective 'jamming,' which basically means rendering the intercept devices totally useless by purposely flooding them with airwaves, is considered practically an act of war in the espionage world... Jamming is reserved for the bad guys."

Plus, the CSE was, and still is, highly dependent on the U.S. for expertise and the latest toys that you just can't get at Future Shop. Instead, the CSE preferred to scramble anything sensitive at its end, which it can explain as a reasonable precaution against any foreign powers listening in.

Occasionally, however, we got our own back on the Americans. In 1981, CSE operators driving a van around Parliament Hill accidently picked up a car phone conversation between the American ambassador and an embassy official. The subject of the chat was their strategy to get a lucrative wheat contract from the Chinese and outbid their strongest competition—the Canadians. Too bad for them that someone was listening, and Canada underbid the U.S. to sell about 12 million metric tonnes of wheat over three years.

Frost also strongly hinted in his book that CSE operators may well have, umm...accidentally listened in to another car phone conversation, where "something good" was "collected."

As a result, Canada secured $50 million in wheat sales to Mexico in 1983.

LEST WE FORGET:
WE'RE WATCHING YOU

AND THE PARANOIA GOES ON, even between friends.

Remember the big brouhaha in late 2006 when the Pentagon's Defense Security Service accused us of planting coins with radio transmitters on their army contractors? Ones who had classified security clearances? By January 2007, Washington did a reversal, saying it was wrong and looking very red-faced...poppy red, you might say. The Associated Press (AP) learned that the Pentagon had got nervous about the specially issued Remembrance Day quarters with the image of a poppy inlaid on the Maple Leaf. What the contractors suspected was "nanotechnology" on the coins turned out to be protective coating the mint had used so the red colouring wouldn't come off!

Years after the flap, the Pentagon couldn't drag its heels anymore and finally had to hand over pertinent emails requested by the AP under the U.S. Freedom of Information Act, though it censored many of them with that convenient catch-all of "national security." In one of the emails, the acting director of counterintelligence wrote: "I don't think it is an issue of the Canadians being the bad guys, but then again, who knows." And at the end of the whole affair, an official expressed the Pentagon's embarrassment in another email: "I am guessing y'all know the status of the Canadian coin situation." (That's right, he actually typed "y'all".) The email suggested an internal meeting "to chat about the next step to put Humpty together again...."

And oh, by the way, the media would have to be contacted, as well as the Canadians.

SIXTEEN
Security

THE OTHER SIDE
IS INSECURE

THE NEXT TIME AMERICANS AT a bar want to lecture you about Canada's supposedly "lax" security, remind them of that hilarious time in 2009 (well, hilarious for everyone else) when the U.S. Transportation Administration (TSA) posted a banquet of sensitive guideline info about airport passenger screening on the Internet. It was done for the convenience of its contractors. The problem was that, if you knew what you were doing, with but a few keystrokes you could get at juicy redacted parts.

The document revealed that certain methods of verifying ID aren't used on all passengers during peak travel crushes. And that certain foreign dignitaries never get screened at all! *Annnnnd*, oh yes, that aircraft flight crew members never get jerked around over those oh-so-annoying restrictions on liquids, gels, aerosols and footwear. And other illuminating gaps in security.

The TSA promptly declared that the document was out of date and the public was never at risk. And while its nose grew longer than the wingspan of a 747, it put five of its staff on administrative leave.

But apparently, security is supposed to be a problem at *our* end. Sure.

Except that, no, the 9/11 terrorists did *not* come down from Canada—they trained at flight schools in the U.S. Moreover, within 45 minutes of the attack, Canada accepted diverted aircraft from the United States, with Gander, Newfoundland, taking in 12,000 confused and frightened people, giving them food and shelter. In Halifax, diverted Americans were offered gourmet meals, and buses took them to a shopping centre where they could buy fresh underwear and toiletries. "The effort here is staggering," Kathy Borrus wrote for the *Washington Post*. "From Gander to the surrounding towns of Norris Arm and Glenwood, our northern neighbours welcomed us."

Naturally, President George W. Bush forgot to say thanks.

Incidentally, 24 Canadians were killed in the attacks on the Twin Towers.

For years, American critics have suggested without any substantiating proof that we're a haven for terrorists. In 2005, former White House official Douglas MacKinnon wrote in the *Washington Times* that our government "not only willingly allows Islamic terrorists into their country but does nothing to stop them from entering our nation." Quoting MacKinnon in her book *Bomb Canada and Other Unkind Remarks in the American Media,* Chantal Allan torpedoes this idiotic reasoning rather pithily by reminding readers, "It seemed to escape MacKinnon's notice that entering the United States required passing through *American* customs checkpoints, not Canadian ones."

Gee, are we "willingly" letting Islamic terrorists into our country? Not if the case of the so-called "Toronto 18" demonstrates anything.

It involved a plot to set off three fertilizer bombs, two in Toronto and one at a military base somewhere in Ontario. Although 7 of the 18 men and youths arrested in 2006 subsequently had their charges dropped or stayed, prompting speculation of police overkill, the threat of the bomb plot was all too terrifyingly real. So far, as we go to press, four men have pleaded guilty to charges, including the charge of participation in a terrorist group. A SWAT team caught two of those who later pleaded guilty red-handed as they unloaded a suspected three tonnes of ammonium nitrate fertilizer from a truck.

Their alleged potential targets included the CN Tower, the Toronto Stock Exchange and the Toronto offices of CSIS. Perhaps nothing brought home the seriousness of the threat more to ordinary Canadians than when video evidence was released of an RCMP-controlled detonation, based on a recipe concocted by one of the ringleaders, Zakaria Amara, for a one-tonne fertilizer bomb. In the video, the Mounties exploded the bomb harmlessly in the middle of a grassy field in Alberta, and the result is grimly impressive—a huge, black cloud spreading from the blast while a nearby steel shipping container is ripped apart and flipped like paper origami. It's easy from the footage to believe police when they say such a bomb in downtown Toronto would have caused "catastrophic damage."

It's clear we're no longer beyond the reach or the consideration of those who think a political point can best be expressed through a spectacle of massive bloodshed. But what's encouraging is that our security forces have so far stopped that spectacle from happening. We do, indeed, have vigilant officers working to make sure terrorism doesn't occur on their watch.

And it's both chilling and tragic that an example exists to demonstrate their commitment.

THE STRANGE
CASE OF PROFESSOR AYERS

FOR THOSE AMERICANS WHO STILL insist we let in any-dangerous-body, consider the odd case of Professor William Ayers from the University of Illinois in Chicago, a leader in educational reform.

Scheduled to speak at the Centre for Urban Schooling at the University of Toronto's Ontario Institute for Studies in Education, Ayers was turned back at the border on a January night in 2009. "I got off the plane like everyone else, and I was asked to come over to the other side," he said. "The border guards reviewed some stuff...If it were me, I would have let me in. I couldn't possibly be a threat to Canada." The border guards also refused to let him see a lawyer brought along to the airport by his host.

Ayers is not just any prof. He travels all over the world, giving lectures on education, and he worked with a little known community activist named Obama on a charity board as well as on Chicago school reform before that same community activist made a bid for the Illinois state Senate in 1995.

So what's the problem? Well, Ayers also happens to have once been a member of the Weather Underground, the 1960s hardcore radical group that declared war on the U.S. government; he contributed to the bombings of New York City Police Headquarters in 1970, the U.S. Capitol building in 1971 and the Pentagon in 1972. He also participated in the "Days of Rage" riots in October 1969. Once upon a time, he was a young man who declared, "Kill all the rich people. Break up their cars and apartments. Bring the revolution home, kill your parents, that's where it's really at."

251

The young radical woman who would later become his wife, Bernardine Dohrn, once joked to an audience about the Charles Manson killings.

Today, of course, Ayers insists he was never a terrorist and is quick to disavow violence, arguing, "We killed no one and hurt no one. Three of our people killed themselves [when bombs they were trying to make blew up in a Greenwich Village townhouse]." When Ayers and Dohrn finally surfaced in 1980 after their fugitive years, the federal charges against them were dropped. A *New York Times* writer in 2001—months before 9/11—was less than impressed with the memoir Ayers wrote, which Ayers admitted was partly fictional, saying he "seems to want to have it both ways, taking responsibility for daring acts in his youth, then deflecting it."

Ayers's past, including his work with Barack Obama made great political ammunition—temporarily—for Sarah Palin when she tried to suggest during the 2008 presidential campaign that the future president chose to "pal around with a terrorist." News organizations went digging, couldn't find the scent of blood and quickly had to conclude that no, Obama didn't have Ayers on his speed dial and never had.

What does all this mean when you come back to an education professor at Pearson Airport in winter? Some ordinary Canadians believe the border guards were right to keep Ayers out, especially when his disavowals of violence appear to be so self-serving and disingenuous, while others argue that Ayers's own government has shelved the matter of his radical past, so it's hardly something for *our* officials to use to prevent his visit to our country. The quick answer to American critics is that no, we don't open the door for everybody. Sometimes we even keep out Americans.

It's quite interesting that as we close in on a decade since 9/11, critics from the south expect us to police their borders for them while the U.S. has not come to terms with its own radical scars, ones that weren't inflicted because of a holy book or a mosque or even a church—but because of economics and a draft. Radical or terrorist, if the individual is born in North America with a Western-sounding name, it seems to change the debate for both liberals and conservatives in both America and Canada.

GOING UNDERGROUND:
CANADA AND NORAD

WE'VE ACTUALLY BEEN HELPING Americans in terms of security ever since our goofy ghost whisperer of a prime minister, Mackenzie King, went behind our backs in 1940 and met Franklin Roosevelt in the president's private railway car in Ogdensburg, New York, signing a joint military agreement. And since 1958, Canadian military personnel have been stationed 950 kilometres from the North Pole at the inhospitable, rugged and shale-covered station of Alert on Ellesmere Island in what is now Nunavut; they used American spy equipment at the site initially to keep watch on the Soviet Union. It's not clear just who they have to keep watch on now.

That same year, we also got together with the Americans to launch NORAD, which has seemed largely irrelevant for the past 20 years except for Santa-tracking and which was suspiciously passive during the 9/11 attacks. A U.S. major told the *Toronto Star* in 2008 that "You'd be surprised" how many fighter jets were scrambled on September 11th, but NORAD wasn't plugged into the FAA's system in 2001, and no shoot-down order was given by the White House.

Also, before Americans bash our supposedly lax security, they might want to remember that 150 of the 900 military personnel working at the Peterson Air Force Base and out of the underground watchtower inside Cheyenne Mountain in Colorado are Canadians (one-and-a-half million tonnes of Canadian explosives actually blew the hole that made their underground base to begin with).

They even have their own hockey team at the base.

SEVENTEEN
Relations

BLOWHARDS AND
BEAVER BARKINGS

IN 2002, CANADIANS HAD TO PUT up with the obnoxious braying of a conservative pundit whose main claims to fame are that his mother, an ethically challenged literary agent, told Linda Tripp to save Monica Lewinsky's stained dress, and that he wrote a book that claimed to find the roots of fascism in liberalism (with the same type of logic that Sir Bedevere in *Monty Python and the Holy Grail* used to find a witch by weighing her against a duck). Oh, and he's also known for bigoted comments about the people of France.

The pundit I'm referring to is the tiresome Jonah Goldberg, whose article for *The National Review,* "Bomb Canada: The Case for War," in reality argued that war wasn't that necessary and that "all Canada needs is to be slapped around a little bit, to be treated like a whining kid who's got to start acting like a man." His complaint stemmed mostly from our refusal to join in the Great Windmill Tilt of 2003, also known as the Iraq War. We'll stand by our military record.

That same year, conservative and former Republican presidential candidate Pat Buchanan called us "Soviet Canuckistan" on his MSNBC show, *Buchanan and Press,* when we grumbled about the way U.S. customs treated our Arab Canadians after 9/11. Of course, Buchanan loses all credibility when you remember this is the guy who worked for Nixon and wrote in a memo about Democratic rival George McGovern that they should "tar him as an extremist." He also suggested Nixon burn the White House tapes.

We've heard worse, of course, from the likes of Ann Coulter (see page 176) and Greg Gutfeld (see page 150).

To be fair, our angriest critics of America don't always appear to be emotionally or intellectually balanced either. When she was a Liberal MP, Carolyn Parrish got caught on camera, fuming, "Damn Americans...I hate those bastards," as she walked away from a scrum. Not smart, and the Tories had a field day with her outburst.

Parrish apologized to Parliament and the U.S. ambassador, but that wasn't the end of her outspokenness. In 2004, she said those who support missile defence are the "coalition of the idiots." She then denied using the word idiot and when faced with the proof asked, "Did I really say idiots? Please, guys, don't put that on tape. I already got into trouble once." Saying *that* to reporters is like flashing a red cape in front of a bull.

Then Prime Minister Paul Martin kicked her out of the caucus after she stomped on a President Bush doll for CBC's *This Hour Has 22 Minutes*.

Even if the Liberals couldn't forgive her, Canadians—feeling their collective gorge rise over Dubya and Iraq—might have. But Parrish's wheels seemed to go off the rails altogether when she lashed out at Chief of Defence Staff Rick Hillier after he commented that the Canadian Forces' "job is to be able to kill people" and called terrorists "murderers and scumbags." Parrish wanted him "muzzled" and complained, "We're sending in armed troops to kill people. This is a drastic change in direction."

Well, no, that happens to be what armies do, and no one entertained the notion that the Taliban would go for a group therapy hug. It's this kind of genuine wing-nut whining that makes rightwing macho American wing-nuts want to slap us.

Five years on, one of our loosest anti-American cannons is now an obscure city councillor in Mississauga.

The truth is that insulting the U.S. should really be left to the professionals. In his segment of "Talking to Americans" for *This Hour Has 22 Minutes*, later expanded into a CBC special for the summer of 2001, Rick Mercer demonstrated that insults work so much better when you get the victims to make themselves look ridiculous through their own ignorance and gullibility.

During the show, among other hysterically funny prank questions, Mercer asked average Americans if the U.S. should bomb Saskatchewan—several thought it should. Respondents at Columbia University, including one professor and a history major, were quite willing to sign a petition discouraging "the Canadian tradition of placing senior citizens on northern ice floes and leaving them to perish." At Stanford University, a top college for science majors, American students readily accepted Mercer's suggestion that Québec doctors "smoke during surgery."

In one of its most famous moments, Mercer told then-presidential candidate George W. Bush back in 2000 that he had achieved an endorsement from Canada's Prime Minister "Jean Poutine." Without missing a beat, Bush said he appreciated the endorsement and that he and "Poutine" would work closely together!

Unlike right-wing critics of Canada, *22 Minutes* at least knows how to be contrite...sort of. In 2003, comedian and actor Colin Mochrie—who achieved his real fame from improvising on the American version of *Whose Line Is it Anyway?*—offered an apology from his alter ego Anthony St. George in Washington, D.C.

"I'm sorry about our waffling on Iraq," Mochrie said during his bit. "I mean, when you're going up against a crazed dictator, you want to have your friends by your side. I realize it took more than two years before you guys pitched in against Hitler, but that was different. Everyone knew he had weapons."

Mochrie closed his piece by saying, "And finally on behalf of all Canadians, I'm sorry that we're constantly apologizing for things in a passive-aggressive way which is really a thinly veiled criticism. I sincerely hope that you're not upset over this. Because we've seen what you do to countries you get upset with."

That's the difference. Insults and satire are funny when there's actual truth contained in them.

WHEN WE'RE ALIKE
AND WHEN WE'RE NOT: THE VANISHING AMERICAN, ENDANGERED AMERICA, THE YANKEE ELEPHANT IN PERIL, BEAVERS WITH SHARP TEETH AND OTHER APOCALYPTIC TITLES

IF WE TRANSPOSED SOME OF THE names of analytical books about our identity to ones for America and its culture, they would sound pretty ridiculous, wouldn't they? They almost conjure images of U.S. citizens hand wringing and waving their arms in the air like so many fleeing Muppets. Sometimes you have to actually pull out the funhouse mirror to get your perspective back.

The truth is that while we've had a steady spate of anaesthetizing, doom-saying books over the decades about the future of our country, more recently we've had controversial books suggesting we're growing more different than the Americans than ever before. Then those new books get criticized, and the seesaw tilts the other way. In his 2007 book *The Unfinished Canadian*, Andrew Cohen tears into the "curious methodology, thinly veiled bias and tiresome self-righteousness" behind the best-selling *Fire and Ice: The United States, Canada and the Myth of Converging Values* by Michael Adams, the co-founder and president of Environics Research and Communications. Cohen wasn't alone in his criticisms of *Fire and Ice*, and he quoted one sociology professor's dismissive review that opined, "At best, this is an op-ed piece spun into a book; at worst, a polemic."

In an insightful chapter, "The American Canadian," Cohen takes us to task for how our own self-righteousness is ingrained (and hey, it permeates this book, too, so he must be right) and how we're closer than we sometimes want to admit to Americans, from say, our Charter of Rights and Freedoms to growing support for the election of senators for fixed terms, instead of having them as appointments lasting until the age of 75. Sometimes Cohen's own examples, of course, can be just as odd as those of his rivals. In terms of elections, he suggests, "Today the major parties allow their leaders no more than two tries (John Turner, Kim Campbell, Joe Clark, Paul Martin) before discarding them...Such intolerance [for losers] is thought to be thoroughly American."

Ehhhhhhhh, wrong. Nobody likes losers. Go to Britain if you want confirmation. After the landslide victory of New Labour in 2001, William Hague quit as leader of the British Conservatives, admitting catastrophic failure. The Tories then brought in Ian Duncan Smith, whose "frog in his throat" and discomfort at the cut and thrust of Parliament got him nicknamed "Ian Duncan Cough." The Tories dumped him in 2003 and brought in Michael Howard. Howard couldn't seal the deal either for the Conservatives in 2005, and out he went, to be replaced by David Cameron. Does all the musical chairs make the British more American? Hardly.

In the early years, in fact, when Hague was still leading the Opposition, the American comparison talk was about how New Labour's Tony Blair may have affected an "American presidential style" and how his wife, Cherie Blair—who had accomplishments in her own right—was the target of much attention as Britain's "First Lady." The chatter didn't last long, even with Blair becoming chums with George Dubya and taking the UK into Iraq. Britain is still Britain, and nobody mistook his slightly frumpy, grumpy successor, Gordon Brown, as being American in style any more than the wife of France's Nicolas Sarkozy, former model Carla Bruni, can be realistically compared with Michelle Obama.

Cohen is fairly balanced in praising some of the virtues of America, particularly in what he calls a "robust, responsive democracy," reminding his readers that Americans "elect representatives to a number of offices, from sheriff to district attorney." Electing law enforcement officials is not something, however, we should be seeking to imitate soon, not when you run the risk of police work left up to the tides of popular opinion.

Americans, Cohen reminds us, "express views on many issues in binding referenda." Yes, they do—so much so that you can be executed in one state but not another, and you can marry your same-sex partner in one state but have this union ignored in another. But Cohen is bang on when he points out that we are guilty of the same sin as Fox News—we think of our neighbour as "a monolith that thinks only one way. It isn't, and it doesn't."

In this book, I have tried to be straightforward in declaring its outlandishly unfair (and fun) bias in our favour, so let's just say the debate over national identities will probably go on forever. But a 2009 book from the big brains behind Ipsos Reid, *We Know What You're Thinking: What Canadians Think and Why*, has an interesting, frank take on the comparison question. Authors Darrell Bricker and John Wright contend that "our two nations have some solid institutional differences," but they don't buy that we're growing increasingly different in values or becoming absorbed. Instead they write, "Many Americans are becoming more like us."

From polls conducted in 1992, 1997 and 2005, Ipsos Reid found that over the years, Americans have grown to feel more like Canadians do in that "the government has a responsibility to take care of the poor" (78 percent of Americans in 2005) and to take care of the elderly (88 percent of Americans in 2005). Their firm also discovered that, five years ago, only 41 percent of

IPSOS REID December 2008 "Global @dvisor" poll

Opinion	Canada (%)	U.S. (%)
Large companies have too much influence on the decisions of my government.	83	84
The government of my country should be more aggressive in regulating the activities of national and multinational corporations.	84	74
Large companies are more powerful than governments.	82	73
Foreign companies have too much control and influence over the economy in my country.	71	71
CEOs of large companies can generally be trusted to tell the truth when they make statements about their company or their industry.	18	17
Government regulation of big businesses and corporations is necessary to protect the public.	73	67
Companies should pay more attention to the environment.	92	84
Companies should do more to contribute to society.	82	78

"The government has a responsibility to take care of the poor."

	Canada (%)	U.S. (%)
1992	83	69
1997	81	61
2005	87	78

"The government has a responsibility to take care of the elderly."

	Canada (%)	U.S. (%)
1992	88	75
1997	87	78
2005	93	88

"People from different racial and cultural backgrounds would be better off it they became more like the majority."

	Canada (%)	U.S. (%)
1992	50	39
1997	44	37
2005	53	41

Americans felt that "people from different racial and cultural backgrounds would be better off if they became more like the majority."

What's most intriguing about these numbers is that they somewhat suggest America's right-wing media is out of touch with a substantial portion of its potential audience. In 2005, long before Barack Obama became president and wound up scolding Wall Street bankers at the White House, Ipsos Reid discovered there was only about a 10-point gap between Canadians and Americans over attitudes toward big business and the banking industry. When it comes to thinking that big companies have too much influence over government, 84 percent of Americans thought they do—compared to 83 percent of Canadians. It's interesting that 74 percent of Americans thought the U.S. government should be more aggressive in regulating such companies. Canadians were also more positive over globalization than Americans (68 percent of Canadians thought it was both a good thing for the world and for Canada, while only 57 percent of Americans thought it was a plus for the planet).

Feeling mischievous, Ipsos Reid asked Canadians during the 2008 federal election whether they'd like Barack Obama as our prime minister. "According to the answers," write Bricker and Wright, "Obama would have easily formed a majority government!"

And despite the long stupor of the Bush years—which gave us Abu Ghraib, the Patriot Act, a vice-president who completely ignored the U.S. Constitution, and a head of state who asked, "Is our children learning?"— we still like our next door neighbour. In 2008, according to Bricker and Wright, 6 out of 10 Canadians liked and admired Americans.

We'll probably like them even better when they grow to be even more like us.

EIGHTEEN
Let's Swap

WE'LL TAKE THESE GUYS, IF YOU'LL TAKE OURS

WHEN IT COMES DOWN TO IT, nationality is an accident of birth. But that doesn't end the "nature or nurture" argument over what makes an American or Canadian. We all know there are certain high-profile individuals who make you wonder if they don't really belong on the other side of the border because of what they say or do.

So this book presents a completely subjective, outrageously unfair but hopefully provocative, controversial and insightful pair of lists, one on Canadians that really belong in the U.S. and should stay there (and most do), and another that is a kind of "wish list" for Americans that many of us would probably be proud to claim as our own.

You Can Have 'Em, America

Rachel Marsden: Canada's Ann Coulter lite, or as *Salon* called her, "Ann Coulter 2.0." Marsden, who insisted to *The Fifth Estate* that Iraq still had weapons of mass destruction long after the Bush regime's claim had been discredited and they had given up on the idea, once suggested on the Fox network that Pakistan cricket fans "should focus less on cricket and a little more on hygiene."

The Vancouver native also once said that morally Canada was like a "Sodom and Gomorrah." This outstandingly moral conservative first achieved a kind of fame when she made controversial date-rape charges against a swim coach at Simon Fraser University; the coach was fired and later reinstated after his counter-claims that she was stalking him. In 1999, a professor at Simon Fraser University went to the police with charges Marsden was stalking him, and in 2004 she pleaded guilty to criminally harassing a former Vancouver radio host.

Having written columns for the *Toronto Sun* and the *New York Post*, she was initially a darling of Fox News, appearing on Bill O'Reilly's rant show and *Red Eye*. Then in 2007, Fox let her go, with security guards escorting her out of the network's New York headquarters, for what an insider told the *Toronto Star* was her erratic behaviour.

Conrad Black: Despite being a proud Anglophile, the Lord of Crossharbour cuts quite an American figure with his very right-wing Yankee attitude. His Gordon Gekko tactics were first revealed to Canadians in a big way in Peter C. Newman's *The Canadian Establishment*. Black wrote a sympathetic biography of Richard Nixon, wrote a bio of Roosevelt that argued the New Deal was a way to save capitalism and confused even British conservatives with his wonky idea that the UK belonged more in NAFTA than the EU.

When he couldn't get a British peerage, he renounced his Canadian citizenship and called ours "an oppressive little world." He changed his tune only after he was indicted for diverting funds and obstructing justice. Please, Lord Black, stay south of the 49th Parallel when you get out of the joint.

Don Cherry: The Mouth that Won't Shut Up. He should go away, not because he is loud or because of those suits he wears that make your eyes bleed, but because the CBC's favourite obnoxious blowhard regularly makes bigoted remarks about Russians, Québécois and "left-wing pinkos." And he actually endorses violent hockey, wanting to get rid of the instigator rule that penalizes a player for starting a fight. For all his vain sartorial displays of supposed patriotism, he appears clueless as to the values of tolerance and informed balance we hold dear in this country.

Any other lout commenting inappropriately on air about foreign affairs or saying Anglophone residents of Sault Ste. Marie "speak the good language" would have been fired, but the CBC has kept Cherry around and even given him a biopic. CBC Sports' own "lexicon" to his egomania and abusive comments helped provide some of the facts on this page—and that in itself is appalling when you think about it.

David Frum: Well, he has been in the U.S. for years, so he might as well stay. The Brahmin child of Canadian journalistic royalty (son of Barbara), Frum went to Harvard law and wound up as a speechwriter for George Dubya (he was once detained by a White House security guard who refused for several minutes to believe a Canadian could have a high-ranking job there). His hero is Alexander Hamilton (yep, the same Al Hamilton who was a spy for the British and who got himself rather foolishly shot in a duel with Aaron Burr) and his favourite American president is Lincoln.

Working now for a conservative think tank, Frum is the most erudite and eloquent spokesperson for the American right, one who—with a Canadian reasonableness—has distanced himself from the Republican name-calling and scare tactics that he calls "outrageous" and "dangerous." America can have him, because America actually *needs* him. He'll inject some much-needed civility and thought into their polarized discourse.

Americans We Wish Could Be Canadians

Al Franken: Once a writer and performer on *Saturday Night Live*, Franken's now a junior senator from

Minnesota who has stood up to the fanatical right and made mincemeat out of them in hilarious books, such as *Rush Limbaugh Is a Big, Fat Idiot and Other Observations.*

He supports universal health care. He got an amendment into the 2010 Defense Appropriations bill that withholds contracts from companies like the engineering and construction firm KBR, "if they restrict their employees from taking workplace sexual assault, battery and discrimination cases to court." (All the "nay" votes against actually protecting workers from sexual assault came from Republicans.) He likes stricter gun control, same-sex marriage and environmental protection—sounds very Canadian, eh?

Gore Vidal: As quintessentially American as he is, being the author of best-selling novels such as *Lincoln* and *Burr,* and having written screenplays and TV shows for Hollywood, Vidal spent many years in self-imposed exile, living in Italy as he wrote essays on the less-flattering aspects of U.S. history and the country's founding. He's a scathing critic of the decline of civilization in general, but even more so of America's icons of Christian fundamentalism and those whom he would consider its priests of prude. He has judged the U.S. sometimes more harshly than even the most anti-American English lit major living in a Kensington Market loft in Toronto. Vidal has called his fellow citizens "the worst-educated people in the First World. They don't have any thoughts, they have emotional responses, which good advertisers know how to provoke."

Americans don't really appreciate the grand old contrarian of their literature, but we could use such an inventive yet pragmatic writer who never lets people forget history.

Janeane Garofalo: Canada could also use the feisty actress and comedian. She can be brutally frank, if not outright disparaging, over the movies she has done. Sounds like our self-deprecating sense of humour. She's informed, shoots from the hip and doesn't consider herself that big a celeb. Sounds very Canadian in her humility. We'd appreciate her wit. She considers the Tea Party protesters racists who are really against Barack Obama in the White House because he's black; to make her point, she once opened one of her stand-up shows with a sarcastic greeting: "If there's any tea baggers here, welcome, and as always, white power."

Gary Larson: Remember the retired cartoonist of *The Far Side*? He must have been separated at birth from the North because his sense of humour is so surreally Canadian. It would have made for one long, fantastic National Film Board cartoon.

Natalie Merchant: No longer as famous and popular as in her early solo album days or as her time as the lead singer of the 10,000 Maniacs, the brunette siren quietly advocates for issues of environmentalism and poverty. She lives in rural New York because she needs to "live where there are more trees than people." We have all the trees she could ever ask for.

Mort Sahl: The comedian and political commentator was actually born in Montréal, but his family soon moved to Los Angeles. Those under 30 have likely never heard of him; those under 40 may have heard of him, but have likely—and sadly—never seen him. But Sahl was to the late 1950s and early 1960s what Bill Maher is today. His ripped-from-the-headlines humour included quips like, "Maybe the Russians will steal our secrets—then they'll be two years behind," and "I'm for capital punishment. You've got to execute people. How else are they going to learn?"

While his views have steered a little to the right with age, he insists on his own website that he's still an iconoclast. ("A Yuppie believes it's courageous to eat in a restaurant that hasn't been reviewed yet.") He should be welcomed home as one of our lost national treasures.

An Epilogue of Compliments

THE GOOD THAT
HOPEFULLY LASTS

THIS WHOLE BOOK IS BASED ON a myth: as in so many other books, it implies throughout that despite the accident of birth that creates nationality, *all* Americans must act in a particular way—whether they're loud, ignorant, war-mongering, xenophobic, they talk before thinking, don't floss their teeth, leave the seat up—because *some* Americans do, or because their government has taken certain actions in its history.

It's the same thing as us kidding ourselves that all Canadians are considerate, tolerant, polite, say "thank you" to vending machines, shovel the patch of sidewalk in front of our house that everyone uses, and that being such *tolerant* people, we'll stop making fun of Newfoundland, honest...in a few minutes.

In this book the beaver tail rests mostly on our side of the scales, which I don't have a problem with, as long as we cop to certain failings; my main criteria was that this book be fun and entertaining.

The bottom line is this: Americans are a great people. Most of us probably just want them to acknowledge now and then that we are as well. But first we have to believe it ourselves. On that score, we're improving. Twenty, maybe even ten years ago, this book, no matter who published it, likely wouldn't have had any credibility for its unabashed pride.

Even though we mentioned it at the start, I wouldn't want this little tome to be taken for an anti-American rant. However the United States has evolved, it was the birthplace of two great ideas, both of which have been elevated in its history to powerful myth—one official and one unofficial. We can't deny, nor should we deny, that they influenced us, so much so that I personally believe these concepts have "matured" in our own society.

The American Declaration of Independence suggested for the first time that citizens had a right to the "pursuit of happiness." Happy? When did a state ever care if its people were happy? The fact that this unique notion got into the text at all was a happy whim of Thomas Jefferson. The inspiration for the revolutionaries' document was, in part, the philosopher John Locke's *Two Treatises of Government*, which argued "no one ought to harm another in his life, health, liberty or possessions." It was Jefferson who took out the idea of property and replaced it with happiness.

Despite the document itself becoming something of a sacred instead of a secular relic for Americans (and for Nicolas Cage to "decode" goofy Freemason ciphers in a trashy thriller) the power of this new way of thinking is a genuine legacy that has inspired people all over the world. Ironically, America's future enemy Ho Chi Minh quoted it when he proclaimed Vietnam's independence from the French in 1945.

Canada, however, is a leader in the world today in recognizing there can be no "pursuit of happiness" unless the government acknowledges other rights. These rights include, for instance, the right to be healthy, and that for the sake of the common good, everyone is entitled to achieve that health and to reach a comfortable old age thanks to equal services; the right, also, to walk down a street without fearing his unstable neighbour is walking around with a Glock 9mm, for which he has no reason to have strapped to his hip except to harm someone.

America reawakened individual liberty. Canada, a land with three vast coastlines, has quietly asserted that no person is an island, that each has a responsibility to his or her brother or sister, and that by pooling our conscience and our efforts, we can best express and enjoy that liberty. We are balancing on the beam more gracefully than we realize, and the world, and lately America, has noticed. At long last, some Americans are contemplating what lessons we might have to offer.

The second great American idea is one that has arguably less basis in fact and more substance in myth. You know the lines: "Give me your tired, your poor, your huddled masses yearning to breathe free." Yes, they're from a poem, but no, contrary to popular belief, they don't appear on the outside of the Statue of Liberty and never have; they're engraved on a bronze plaque inside. Not hidden, mind you, but tucked away, a placement that's symbolic of certain nagging contradictions. The myth is that America welcomes immigrants fleeing poverty and political oppression, despite Congress passing the Chinese Exclusion Act of 1882 and the Immigration Act of 1924, and despite that Americans of older Anglo stock liked to routinely persecute these new immigrants as they came in by the thousands through Ellis Island.

In truth, immigrants could come in for a long time, because no one could suggest that apart from Natives, there was an "original" people there. And in truth, the city of London, England, was a haven for political dissidents from abroad long before New York and other U.S. cities were—not because it welcomed them, mind you, but because these gadflies sought the shelter of British democratic institutions and English law. Karl Marx wrote for a while for the *New York Tribune*, but he spent years of his life in London.

But back to that great idea, because what is important about the talk of those "huddled masses" is that for the first time, a country incorporated into its sense of being the notion that people should come to a new land and be welcomed for their own reasons—not to serve the purpose of its government or inhabitants. It's an idea that even Canada didn't acknowledge and adopt in spirit until the late 1970s; after all, multiculturalism was invented first as a political ploy to subvert Québec separatism.

It can be argued, though, that we are the true inheritors and practitioners of this spirit today, accepting immigrants of every shade or creed not only as policy but as a value of our nation (though we prefer well-to-do immigrants, and an engineering degree wouldn't hurt).

Today, the U.S. still battles with itself over its immigration realities, knowing full well that its economy owes a lot to illegal aliens working jobs that its citizens with full rights don't, while some citizens would like to erect a wall barring Mexico (and perhaps a wall for us, too). Up here, we have finally come around to the idea that as the second biggest country on Earth, we have the room to be compassionate. It took us an embarrassingly long time, but we got there.

This sounds like a backhanded way of complimenting ourselves instead of complimenting America. But a philosophical debt is owed. That supposedly constant, polite Canadian hand should always be extended in friendship, even if it gets slapped away now and then. We don't put it out there because we need the Americans. We do it because it's the right thing to do. In writing this book, I kept diving—and not by choice—into the polarization of left and right going on in America today, one in which the right keeps using us as a bogeyman and whipping boy. You can't help but think Bricker and Wright of Ipsos Reid are on to something when they suggest, "Many

Americans are becoming more like us." It explains a lot about why we've been vilified during the discourse. The scare tactics are used by those who aren't like us and who never want to be—those who have the most to fear and who have the most to lose.

So if America is evolving into Canada, those gloomy and infuriatingly dull, pontificating books of the past remaindered in store discount bins were always wrong. We have a shared destiny, one more interesting, more unpredictable and with luck, more prosperous than anyone could have guessed. I argued earlier in these pages that a shared currency is nothing to fear. Europe does quite nicely with one. And citizens of the EU, whether from Britain, Spain, Germany, wherever in the union, can cross borders to work in another member country. This, indeed, is our next hurdle, because governments have made life more convenient for corporations, making trade free, but not making it easier for individuals to live and work where we prefer.

All jokes, all ribbing aside, there is no jingoistic identity for a beaver or an eagle. There are simply human beings on a vast continent who come in every shade of creative brilliance and stupid, vain ignorance, of private doubt and restless yearning for accomplishment and security. Throughout this book, I have been discussing two interconnected heritages, and whatever it says on our birth certificates or citizenship documents, the reality is we still have much to teach each other. And we can help each other. We ought to get on with that.

It sounds very high-minded and almost naïve, but after all, it was written by a Canadian.

Selected References

Allan, Chantal. *Bomb Canada and Other Unkind Remarks in the American Media*. Edmonton, AB: AU Press, 2009.

Berton, Pierre. *Marching as to War*. Toronto, ON: Anchor Canada, 2002 reprint edition.

Bisson, James. *One Hundred Greatest Canadian Sports Moments*. Toronto, ON: Wiley & Sons Canada, 2008.

Bricker, Darrell and John Wright. *We Know What You're Thinking: What Canadians Think and Why*. Toronto, ON: HarperCollins, 2009.

Cohen, Andrew. *The Unfinished Canadian*. Toronto, ON: McClelland & Stewart, 2007.

Cole, J. Michael. *Smokescreen: Canadian Security Intelligence after September 11, 2001*. Bloomington, IN: iUniverse, 2008.

Frost, Mike and Michel Gratton. *Spyworld: Inside the Canadian and American Intelligence Establishments*. Toronto, ON: Doubleday, 1994.

Ganser, Daniele. *NATO's Secret Armies: Operation Gladio and Terrorism in Western Europe*. New York, NY: Frank Cass, 2005.

Gilmour, Don, Achille Michaud and Pierre Turgeon. *A People's History of Canada, Volumes One and Two*. Toronto, ON: McClelland and Stewart, 2000.

Granatstein, J.L. *Who Killed Canadian History?* Revised ed. Toronto, ON: HarperCollins, 2007.

Granatstein, J.L. *Yankee Go Home? Canadians and Anti-Americanism*. Toronto, ON: HarperCollins, 1996.

Hurtig, Mel. *The Truth About Canada: Some important, some astonishing, and some truly appalling things all Canadians should know about our country*. Toronto, ON: McClelland & Stewart, 2008.

Latimer, Jon. *1812: War with America*. Cambridge, UK: Belknap Press, 2007.

Jones, David T. and David Kilgour. *Uneasy Neighbours: Canada, the USA and the Dynamics of State, Industry and Culture*. Toronto, ON: Wiley & Sons Canada, 2007.

Karnow, Stanley. *Vietnam: A History*. New York, NY: Penguin Books, 1997 reprint edition.

Morton, Desmond. *A Military History of Canada*. 5th ed. Toronto, ON: McClelland & Stewart, 2007.

Pigott, Peter. *Canada in Afghanistan: The War So Far*. Toronto, ON: Dundurn Press, 2007.

Pigott, Peter. *Canada in Sudan: War Without Borders*. Toronto, ON: Dundurn Press, 2009.

Sawatsky, John. *Men in the Shadows: The RCMP Security Service*. Toronto, ON: Doubleday, 1980.

Vidal, Gore. *Inventing a Nation: Washington, Adams, Jefferson*. New Haven, CT: Yale University Press, 2003.

Volkomer, Walter E. *American Government*. 11th ed. Upper Saddle River, NJ: Pearson Prentice Hall, 2007.

Watson, Patrick and Hugh Graham. *The Canadians: Biographies of a Nation*. Omnibus ed. Toronto, ON: McArthur & Company, 2003.

"The Best Place on Earth: Canada versus the World." *Maclean's*, July 6, 2009.

"Canada's Biggest Problem? America." *Maclean's*, October 12, 2009

About the Author

Jeff Pearce has written shamelessly on a variety of things he knows nothing about. He was a farm reporter in Saskatchewan without ever seeing a farm, wrote an article on trucking brakes when he can't drive, has ghost-written editorials for an Indian community newspaper when he can't claim any roots to Delhi or Mumbai and edited financial magazines in London, England, when he can't do simple multiplication. In this book, however, he actually got to put to paper the rants he's been having with himself, his family, his friends and total strangers for years! So, he is certainly qualified to cover the range of subjects in this book. He has worked as a writer for both TV and magazines, and he has nine novels and two non-fiction titles published, some under pseudonyms, in Canada, the U.S. and the UK.